D0149985

Essay on Man
and Other Poems

DOVER · THRIFT · EDITIONS

Essay on Man
and Other Poems

ALEXANDER POPE

DOVER PUBLICATIONS, INC.
New York

DOVER THRIFT EDITIONS

Editor: Stanley Appelbaum

Copyright

Copyright © 1994 by Dover Publications, Inc.
All rights reserved.

Bibliographical Note

This Dover edition, first published in 1994, is a new selection of unabridged poems reprinted from a standard text. A new Note, lists of titles and first lines, and footnotes have been prepared specially for the present edition.

Library of Congress Cataloging-in-Publication Data

Pope, Alexander, 1688–1744.
    Essay on man and other poems / Alexander Pope.
        p.   cm. — (Dover thrift editions)
    Includes indexes.
    Contents: Ode on solitude — The dying Christian to his soul — Elegy to the memory of an unfortunate lady — An essay on criticism — The rape of the lock — Essay on man — Epistle IV — Epistle to Dr. Arbuthnot — Epigram: engraved on the collar of a dog.
    ISBN-13: 978-0-486-28053-0 (pbk.)
    ISBN-10: 0-486-28053-5 (pbk.)
    I. Title.   II. Title: Essay on man.   III. Series.
PR3622   1994
821'.5 — dc20   93-42205
                                                                                   CIP

Manufactured in the United States by Courier Corporation
28053510   2015
www.doverpublications.com

Note

ALEXANDER POPE (1688–1744), chief poet of the Augustan age, is one of the greatest and most frequently quoted English writers. His perfection of expression and exquisite taste in prosody are legendary, as is his wide range of moods from heartfelt elegy to merciless satire. The present selection includes, absolutely uncut, three long poems—the serious disquisitions "An Essay on Criticism" and "Essay on Man" and the mock-epic "The Rape of the Lock"—in addition to seven other varied works. The epistle to the Earl of Burlington displays much of the poet's interest in architecture and landscaping. The epistle to Dr. Arbuthnot reveals much of his private life and feelings.

The footnotes added here are limited in scope. No attempt has been made to identify mythological and major historical names readily locatable in standard reference books; on the other hand, oblique references to such characters have been explained briefly and less familiar names have been identified. Pope's nicknames or pseudonyms for actual contemporaries have not been glossed; the points he is making are generally clear from the context.

Contents

The years are those of first publication, where available.

Essay on Man
and Other Poems

Ode on Solitude

Happy the man, whose wish and care
 A few paternal acres bound,
Content to breathe his native air
            In his own ground.

Whose herds with milk, whose fields with bread,
 Whose flocks supply him with attire,
Whose trees in summer yield him shade,
            In winter fire.

Blest, who can unconcern'dly find
 Hours, days, and years slide soft away,
In health of body, peace of mind,
            Quiet by day.

Sound sleep by night; study and ease,
 Together mixt; sweet recreation:
And innocence, which most does please
            With meditation.

Thus let me live, unseen, unknown,
 Thus unlamented let me die,
Steal from the world, and not a stone
            Tell where I lie.

The Dying Christian to His Soul

Ode

1   Vital spark of heavenly flame!
        Quit, oh quit this mortal frame!
        Trembling, hoping, lingering, flying,
        Oh the pain, the bliss of dying!
       Cease, fond Nature, cease thy strife,
       And let me languish into life!

1

II Hark! they whisper; angels say,
  "Sister Spirit, come away!"
  What is this absorbs me quite?
  Steals my senses, shuts my sight,
Drowns my spirits, draws my breath?
Tell me, my Soul, can this be death?

III The world recedes; it disappears!
  Heaven opens on my eyes! my ears
   With sounds seraphic ring:
  Lend, lend your wings! I mount! I fly!
  O Grave! where is thy victory?
   O Death! where is thy sting?

Elegy

TO THE MEMORY OF AN UNFORTUNATE LADY

What beckoning ghost along the moonlight shade
Invites my steps, and points to yonder glade?
'Tis she! — but why that bleeding bosom gored,
Why dimly gleams the visionary sword?
Oh, ever beauteous, ever friendly! tell,
Is it, in heaven, a crime to love too well?
To bear too tender or too firm a heart,
To act a lover's or a Roman's part?
Is there no bright reversion in the sky
For those who greatly think, or bravely die?
 Why bade ye else, ye powers! her soul aspire
Above the vulgar flight of low desire?
Ambition first sprung from your blest abodes,
The glorious fault of angels and of gods:
Thence to their images on earth it flows,
And in the breast of kings and heroes glows.
Most souls, 'tis true, but peep out once an age,
Dull, sullen prisoners in the body's cage:
Dim lights of life, that burn a length of years,
Useless, unseen, as lamps in sepulchres;
Like Eastern kings a lazy state they keep,
And, close confined to their own palace, sleep.

From these perhaps (ere Nature bade her die)
Fate snatched her early to the pitying sky.
As into air the purer spirits flow,
And separate from their kindred dregs below;
So flew the soul to its congenial place,
Nor left one virtue to redeem her race,
    But thou, false guardian of a charge too good,
Thou, mean deserter of thy brother's blood!
See on these ruby lips the trembling breath,
These cheeks now fading at the blast of death;
Cold is that breast which warm'd the world before,
And those love-darting eyes must roll no more.
Thus, if eternal justice rules the ball,
Thus shall your wives, and thus your children fall:
On all the line a sudden vengeance waits,
And frequent hearses shall besiege your gates;
There passengers shall stand, and pointing say,
(While the long funerals blacken all the way,)
"Lo! these were they, whose souls the Furies steel'd,
And cursed with hearts unknowing how to yield."
    Thus unlamented pass the proud away,
The gaze of fools, and pageant of a day!
So perish all, whose breast ne'er learn'd to glow
For others' good, or melt at others' woe.
    What can atone (oh ever-injured shade!)
Thy fate unpitied, and thy rites unpaid?
No friend's complaint, no kind domestic tear
Pleased thy pale ghost, or graced thy mournful bier.
By foreign hands thy dying eyes were closed,
By foreign hands thy decent limbs composed,
By foreign hands thy humble grave adorn'd,
By strangers honour'd, and by strangers mourn'd!
What, though no friends in sable weeds appear,
Grieve for an hour, perhaps then mourn a year,
And bear about the mockery of woe
To midnight dances, and the public show?
What, though no weeping loves thy ashes grace,
Nor polish'd marble emulate thy face?
What, though no sacred earth allow thee room,
Nor hallow'd dirge be mutter'd o'er thy tomb?
Yet shall thy grave with rising flowers be dress'd

And the green turf lie lightly on thy breast:
There shall the morn her earliest tears bestow,
There the first roses of the year shall blow;
While angels with their silver wings o'ershade
The ground now sacred by thy reliques made.
   So peaceful rests, without a stone, a name,
What once had beauty, titles, wealth, and fame.
How loved, how honour'd once, avails thee not,
To whom related, or by whom begot;
A heap of dust alone remains of thee,
'Tis all thou art, and all the proud shall be!
   Poets themselves must fall, like those they sung,
Deaf the praised ear, and mute the tuneful tongue.
Even he, whose soul now melts in mournful lays,
Shall shortly want the generous tear he pays;
Then from his closing eyes thy form shall part,
And the last pang shall tear thee from his heart,
Life's idle business at one gasp be o'er,
The Muse forgot, and thou beloved no more!

An Essay on Criticism

I

'Tis hard to say, if greater want of skill
Appear in writing or in judging ill;
But, of the two, less dangerous is the offence
To tire our patience, than mislead our sense.
Some few in that, but numbers err in this,
Ten censure wrong for one who writes amiss;
A fool might once himself alone expose,
Now one in verse makes many more in prose.
   'Tis with our judgments as our watches, none
Go just alike, yet each believes his own.
In poets as true genius is but rare,
True taste as seldom is the critic's share,
Both must alike from Heaven derive their light,
These born to judge, as well as those to write.
Let such teach others who themselves excel,
And censure freely who have written well.

Authors are partial to their wit, 'tis true,
But are not critics to their judgment too?
  Yet, if we look more closely, we shall find
Most have the seeds of judgment in their mind:
Nature affords at least a glimmering light;
The lines, though touch'd but faintly, are drawn right.
But as the slightest sketch, if justly traced,
Is by ill colouring but the more disgraced,
So by false learning is good sense defaced;
Some are bewilder'd in the maze of schools,
And some made coxcombs Nature meant but fools.
In search of wit these lose their common sense,
And then turn critics in their own defence:
Each burns alike, who can, or cannot write,
Or with a rival's, or an eunuch's spite.
All fools have still an itching to deride,
And fain would be upon the laughing side.
If Mævius scribble in Apollo's spite,
There are who judge still worse than he can write.
  Some have at first for wits, then poets pass'd,
Turn'd critics next, and proved plain fools at last.
Some neither can for wits nor critics pass,
As heavy mules are neither horse nor ass.
Those half-learn'd witlings, numerous in our isle,
As half-form'd insects on the banks of Nile;
Unfinish'd things, one knows not what to call,
Their generation's so equivocal:
To tell them would a hundred tongues require,
Or one vain wit's, that might a hundred tire.
  But you who seek to give and merit fame,
And justly bear a critic's noble name,
Be sure yourself and your own reach to know,
How far your genius, taste, and learning go;
Launch not beyond your depth, but be discreet,
And mark that point where sense and dulness meet.
  Nature to all things fix'd the limits fit,
And wisely curb'd proud man's pretending wit.
As on the land while here the ocean gains,
In other parts it leaves wide sandy plains;
Thus in the soul while memory prevails,
The solid power of understanding fails;
Where beams of warm imagination play,

The memory's soft figures melt away.
One science only will one genius fit:
So vast is art, so narrow human wit:
Not only bounded to peculiar arts,
But oft in those confined to single parts.
Like kings we lose the conquests gain'd before,
By vain ambition still to make them more:
Each might his servile province well command,
Would all but stoop to what they understand.
    First follow Nature, and your judgment frame
By her just standard, which is still the same:
Unerring Nature, still divinely bright,
One clear, unchanged, and universal light,
Life, force, and beauty, must to all impart,
At once the source, and end, and test of Art.
Art from that fund each just supply provides;
Works without show, and without pomp presides:
In some fair body thus th' informing soul
With spirits feeds, with vigour fills the whole,
Each motion guides, and every nerve sustains;
Itself unseen, but in th' effects remains.
Some, to whom Heaven in wit has been profuse,
Want as much more to turn it to its use;
For wit and judgment often are at strife,
Though meant each other's aid, like man and wife.
'Tis more to guide, than spur the Muse's steed;
Restrain his fury, than provoke his speed:
The winged courser, like a generous horse,
Shows most true mettle when you check his course.
    Those rules of old discover'd, not devised,
Are Nature still, but Nature methodised:
Nature, like liberty, is but restrain'd
By the same laws which first herself ordain'd.
    Hear how learn'd Greece her useful rules indites,
When to repress, and when indulge our flights:
High on Parnassus' top her sons she show'd,
And pointed out those arduous paths they trod;
Held from afar, aloft, the immortal prize,
And urged the rest by equal steps to rise.
Just precepts thus from great examples given,
She drew from them what they derive from Heaven.

The generous critic fann'd the poet's fire,
And taught the world with reason to admire.
Then criticism the Muse's handmaid proved,
To dress her charms, and make her more beloved:
But following wits from that intention stray'd,
Who could not win the mistress, woo'd the maid;
Against the poets their own arms they turn'd,
Sure to hate most the men from whom they learn'd.
So modern 'pothecaries, taught the art
By doctor's bills to play the doctor's part,
Bold in the practice of mistaken rules,
Prescribe, apply, and call their masters fools.
Some on the leaves of ancient authors prey,
Nor time nor moths e'er spoil'd so much as they:
Some drily plain, without invention's aid,
Write dull receipts how poems may be made.
These leave the sense, their learning to display,
And those explain the meaning quite away.

    You then whose judgment the right course would steer,
Know well each Ancient's proper character:
His fable, subject, scope in every page;
Religion, country, genius of his age:
Without all these at once before your eyes,
Cavil you may, but never criticise.
Be Homer's works your study and delight,
Read them by day, and meditate by night;
Thence form your judgment, thence your maxims bring,
And trace the Muses upward to their spring.
Still with itself compared, his text peruse;
And let your comment be the Mantuan Muse.[1]

    When first young Maro[1] in his boundless mind
A work to outlast immortal Rome design'd,
Perhaps he seem'd above the critic's law,
And but from Nature's fountains scorn'd to draw:
But when to examine every part he came,
Nature and Homer were, he found, the same.
Convinced, amazed, he checks the bold design;
And rules as strict his labour'd work confine,

---

[1] Vergil (Publius Vergilius Maro, of Mantua).

As if the Stagyrite[2] o'erlook'd each line.
Learn hence for ancient rules a just esteem;
To copy Nature is to copy them.
  Some beauties yet no precepts can declare,
For there's a happiness as well as care.
Music resembles poetry, in each
Are nameless graces which no methods teach,
And which a master-hand alone can reach.
If, where the rules not far enough extend,
(Since rules were made but to promote their end)
Some lucky licence answer to the full
The intent proposed, that licence is a rule.
Thus Pegasus, a nearer way to take,
May boldly deviate from the common track.
Great wits sometimes may gloriously offend,
And rise to faults true critics dare not mend;
From vulgar bounds with brave disorder part,
And snatch a grace beyond the reach of art,
Which, without passing through the judgment, gains
The heart, and all its end at once attains.
In prospects thus, some objects please our eyes,
Which out of Nature's common order rise,
The shapeless rock, or hanging precipice.
But though the ancients thus their rules invade,
(As kings dispense with laws themselves have made)
Moderns, beware! or if you must offend
Against the precept, ne'er transgress its end;
Let it be seldom, and compell'd by need;
And have, at least, their precedent to plead.
The critic else proceeds without remorse,
Seizes your fame, and puts his laws in force.
  I know there are, to whose presumptuous thoughts
Those freer beauties, even in them, seem faults.
Some figures monstrous and misshaped appear,
Consider'd singly, or beheld too near,
Which, but proportion'd to their light, or place,
Due distance reconciles to form and grace.

---

[2] Aristotle.

A prudent chief not always must display
His powers, in equal ranks, and fair array,
But with the occasion and the place comply,
Conceal his force, nay seem sometimes to fly.
Those oft are stratagems which errors seem,
Nor is it Homer nods, but we that dream.
  Still green with bays each ancient altar stands,
Above the reach of sacrilegious hands;
Secure from flames, from envy's fiercer rage,
Destructive war, and all-involving age.
See from each clime the learn'd their incense bring!
Hear in all tongues consenting pæans ring!
In praise so just let every voice be join'd,
And fill the general chorus of mankind.
Hail, bards triumphant! born in happier days;
Immortal heirs of universal praise!
Whose honours with increase of ages grow,
As streams roll down, enlarging as they flow;
Nations unborn your mighty names shall sound,
And worlds applaud that must not yet be found!
O may some spark of your celestial fire,
The last, the meanest of your sons inspire,
(That on weak wings, from far, pursues your flights;
Glows while he reads, but trembles as he writes)
To teach vain wits a science little known,
To admire superior sense, and doubt their own!

II

Of all the causes which conspire to blind
Man's erring judgment, and misguide the mind,
What the weak head with strongest bias rules,
Is PRIDE, the never-failing vice of fools.
Whatever Nature has in worth denied,
She gives in large recruits of needless pride;
For as in bodies, thus in souls we find
What wants in blood and spirits, swell'd with wind:
Pride, where wit fails, steps in to our defence,
And fills up all the mighty void of sense.
If once right reason drives that cloud away,
Truth breaks upon us with resistless day.
Trust not yourself; but your defects to know,

Make use of every friend — and every foe.
A little learning is a dangerous thing;
Drink deep, or taste not the Pierian spring:[3]
There shallow draughts intoxicate the brain,
And drinking largely sobers us again.
Fired at first sight with what the Muse imparts,
In fearless youth we tempt the height of arts,
While from the bounded level of our mind,
Short views we take, nor see the lengths behind;
But more advanced, behold with strange surprise
New distant scenes of endless science rise!
So pleased at first the towering Alps we try,
Mount o'er the vales, and seem to tread the sky,
The eternal snows appear already passed,
And the first clouds and mountains seem the last:
But, those attain'd, we tremble to survey
The growing labours of the lengthen'd way,
The increasing prospect tires our wandering eyes,
Hills peep o'er hills, and Alps on Alps arise!
    A perfect judge will read each work of wit
With the same spirit that its author writ:
Survey the WHOLE, nor seeks slight faults to find
Where Nature moves, and rapture warms the mind,
Nor lose, for that malignant dull delight,
The generous pleasure to be charm'd with wit.
But in such lays as neither ebb nor flow,
Correctly cold, and regularly low,
That shunning faults, one quiet tenor keep;
We cannot blame indeed — but we may sleep.
In wit, as Nature, what affects our hearts
Is not th' exactness of peculiar parts;
'Tis not a lip, or eye, we beauty call,
But the joint force and full result of all.
Thus when we view some well-proportion'd dome,
(The world's just wonder, and ev'n thine, O Rome!)
No single parts unequally surprise,
All comes united to th' admiring eyes;

---

[3] On Mount Parnassus, home of the Muses.

No monstrous height, or breadth or length appear;
The whole at once is bold and regular.
    Whoever thinks a faultless piece to see,
Thinks what ne'er was, nor is, nor e'er shall be,
In every work regard the writer's end,
Since none can compass more than they intend;
And if the means be just, the conduct true,
Applause, in spite of trivial faults, is due.
As men of breeding, sometimes men of wit,
To avoid great errors, must the less commit:
Neglect the rules each verbal critic lays,
For not to know some trifles, is a praise.
Most critics, fond of some subservient art,
Still make the whole depend upon a part:
They talk of principles, but notions prize,
And all to one loved folly sacrifice.
    Once on a time, La Mancha's knight, they say
A certain bard encountering on the way,
Discoursed in terms as just, with looks as sage,
As e'er could Dennis,[4] of the Grecian stage;
Concluding all were desperate sots and fools,
Who durst depart from Aristotle's rules.
Our author, happy in a judge so nice,
Produced his play, and begg'd the knight's advice;
Made him observe the subject and the plot,
The manners, passions, unities; what not?
All which, exact to rule, were brought about,
Were but a combat in the lists left out.
"What! leave the combat out?" exclaims the knight;
Yes, or we must renounce the Stagyrite.
"Not so, by heaven, (he answers in a rage)
"Knights, squires, and steeds, must enter on the stage."
So vast a throng the stage can ne'er contain.
"Then build a new, or act it in a plain."
    Thus critics of less judgment than caprice,
Curious, not knowing, not exact but nice,
Form short ideas; and offend in arts

---

[4] The critic John Dennis, an adversary of Pope.

(As most in manners) by a love to parts.
    Some to Conceit alone their taste confine,
And glittering thoughts struck out at every line;
Pleased with a work where nothing's just or fit;
One glaring chaos and wild heap of wit.
Poets, like painters, thus, unskill'd to trace
The naked Nature and the living grace,
With gold and jewels cover every part,
And hide with ornaments their want of art.
True wit is Nature to advantage dress'd;
What oft was thought, but ne'er so well express'd;
Something, whose truth convinced at sight we find,
That gives us back the image of our mind.
As shades more sweetly recommend the light,
So modest plainness sets off sprightly wit.
For works may have more wit than does 'em good,
As bodies perish through excess of blood.
    Others for Language all their care express,
And value books, as women men, for dress:
Their praise is still, — The style is excellent;
The sense, they humbly take upon content.
Words are like leaves; and where they most abound,
Much fruit of sense beneath is rarely found.
False eloquence, like the prismatic glass,
Its gaudy colours spreads on every place;
The face of Nature we no more survey,
All glares alike, without distinction gay:
But true expression, like th' unchanging sun,
Clears and improves whate'er it shines upon,
It gilds all objects, but it alters none.
Expression is the dress of thought, and still
Appears more decent, as more suitable;
A vile conceit in pompous words express'd
Is like a clown in regal purple dress'd:
For different styles with different subjects sort,
As several garbs, with country, town, and court.
Some by old words to fame have made pretence,
Ancients in phrase, mere moderns in their sense;
Such labour'd nothings, in so strange a style,
Amaze the unlearn'd, and make the learned smile.
Unlucky as Fungoso in the play,

These sparks with awkward vanity display
What the fine gentleman wore yesterday;
And but so mimic ancient wits at best,
As apes our grandsires, in their doublets dress'd.
In words, as fashions, the same rule will hold;
Alike fantastic, if too new, or old:
Be not the first by whom the new are tried,
Nor yet the last to lay the old aside.
  But most by numbers judge a poet's song:
And smooth or rough, with them, is right or wrong:
In the bright muse, though thousand charms conspire,
Her voice is all these tuneful fools admire;
Who haunt Parnassus but to please their ear,
Not mend their minds; as some to church repair,
Not for the doctrine, but the music there.
These equal syllables alone require,
Though oft the ear the open vowels tire;
While expletives their feeble aid do join;
And ten low words oft creep in one dull line:
While they ring round the same unvaried chimes,
With sure returns of still expected rhymes;
Where'er you find "the cooling western breeze,"
In the next line, it "whispers through the trees":
If crystal streams "with pleasing murmurs creep":
The reader's threaten'd (not in vain) with "sleep."
Then, at the last and only couplet fraught
With some unmeaning thing they call a thought,
A needless Alexandrine ends the song,
That, like a wounded snake, drags its slow length along.
Leave such to tune their own dull rhymes, and know
What's roundly smooth, or languishingly slow;
And praise the easy vigour of a line,
Where Denham's[5] strength, and Waller's sweetness join.
True ease in writing comes from art, not chance,
As those move easiest who have learn'd to dance.
'Tis not enough no harshness gives offence,
The sound must seem an echo to the sense:
Soft is the strain when Zephyr gently blows,

---

[5] John Denham, seventeenth-century poet.

And the smooth stream in smoother numbers flows;
But when loud billows lash the sounding shore,
The hoarse, rough verse should like the torrent roar.
When Ajax strives some rock's vast weight to throw,
The line too labours, and the words move slow:
Not so, when swift Camilla scours the plain,
Flies o'er the unbending corn, and skims along the main.
Hear how Timotheus' varied lays surprise,
And bid alternate passions fall and rise!
While, at each change, the son of Libyan Jove
Now burns with glory, and then melts with love;
Now his fierce eyes with sparkling fury glow,
Now sighs steal out, and tears begin to flow:
Persians and Greeks like turns of Nature found,
And the world's victor stood subdued by sound!
The power of music all our hearts allow,
And what Timotheus was, is DRYDEN now.

   Avoid extremes; and shun the fault of such,
Who still are pleased too little or too much.
At every trifle scorn to take offence,
That always shows great pride, or little sense;
Those heads, as stomachs, are not sure the best,
Which nauseate all, and nothing can digest.
Yet let not each gay turn thy rapture move;
For fools admire, but men of sense approve:
As things seem large which we through mists descry,
Dulness is ever apt to magnify.

   Some foreign writers, some our own despise;
The ancients only, or the moderns prize.
Thus wit, like faith, by each man is applied
To one small sect, and all are damn'd beside.
Meanly they seek the blessing to confine,
And force that sun but on a part to shine,
Which not alone the southern wit sublimes,
But ripens spirits in cold northern climes;
Which from the first has shone on ages past,
Enlights the present, and shall warm the last;
Though each may feel increases and decays,
And see now clearer and now darker days.
Regard not then if wit be old or new,
But blame the false, and value still the true.

Some ne'er advance a judgment of their own,
But catch the spreading notion of the town;
They reason and conclude by precedent,
And own stale nonsense which they ne'er invent.
Some judge of authors' names, not works, and then
Nor praise nor blame the writings, but the men.
Of all this servile herd, the worst is he
That in proud dulness joins with quality,
A constant critic at the great man's board,
To fetch and carry nonsense for my lord.
What woful stuff this madrigal would be,
In some starved hackney sonnetteer, or me?
But let a lord once own the happy lines,
How the wit brightens! how the style refines!
Before his sacred name flies every fault,
And each exalted stanza teems with thought!
    The vulgar thus through imitation err;
As oft the learn'd by being singular;
So much they scorn the crowd, that if the throng
By chance go right, they purposely go wrong:
So schismatics the plain believers quit,
And are but damn'd for having too much wit.
Some praise at morning what they blame at night;
But always think the last opinion right.
A Muse by these is like a mistress used,
This hour she's idolized, the next abused;
While their weak heads, like towns unfortified,
'Twixt sense and nonsense daily change their side.
Ask them the cause; they're wiser still, they say;
And still to-morrow's wiser than to-day.
We think our fathers fools, so wise we grow;
Our wiser sons, no doubt, will think us so.
Once school-divines this zealous isle o'erspread;
Who knew most sentences, was deepest read:
Faith, Gospel, all seem'd made to be disputed.
And none had sense enough to be confuted:
Scotists and Thomists, now in peace remain,
Amidst their kindred cobwebs in Duck-lane.[6]

---

[6] A London street of secondhand book dealers.

If Faith itself has different dresses worn,
What wonder modes in wit should take their turn?
Oft leaving what is natural and fit,
The current folly proves the ready wit;
And authors think their reputation safe,
Which lives as long as fools are pleased to laugh.
  Some valuing those of their own side or mind,
Still make themselves the measure of mankind:
Fondly we think we honour merit then,
When we but praise ourselves in other men.
Parties in wit attend on those of state,
And public faction doubles private hate.
Pride, malice, folly, against Dryden rose,
In various shapes of parsons, critics, beaus;
But sense survived when merry jests were past;
For rising merit will buoy up at last.
Might he return, and bless once more our eyes,
New Blackmores and new Milbourns must arise:
Nay, should great Homer lift his awful head,
Zoilus again would start up from the dead.
Envy will merit, as its shade, pursue;
But like a shadow, proves the substance true:
For envied wit, like Sol eclipsed, makes known
The opposing body's grossness, not its own.
When first that sun too powerful beams displays,
It draws up vapours which obscure its rays;
But even those clouds at last adorn its way,
Reflect new glories, and augment the day.
  Be thou the first true merit to befriend;
His praise is lost, who stays till all commend.
Short is the date, alas! of modern rhymes,
And 'tis but just to let them live betimes.
No longer now that golden age appears,
When patriarch-wits survived a thousand years:
Now length of fame (our second life) is lost,
And bare threescore is all even that can boast;
Our sons their fathers' failing language see,
And such as Chaucer is, shall Dryden be.
So when the faithful pencil has design'd
Some bright idea of the master's mind,
Where a new word leaps out at his command,

And ready Nature waits upon his hand;
When the ripe colours soften and unite,
And sweetly melt into just shade and light;
When mellow years their full perfection give,
And each bold figure just begins to live,
The treacherous colours the fair art betray,
And all the bright creation fades away!
    Unhappy wit, like most mistaken things,
Atones not for that envy which it brings.
In youth alone its empty praise we boast,
But soon the short-lived vanity is lost:
Like some fair flower the early spring supplies,
That gaily blooms, but even in blooming dies.
What is this wit, which must our cares employ?
The owner's wife, that other men enjoy;
Then most our trouble still when most admired,
And still the more we give, the more required;
Whose fame with pains we guard, but lose with ease,
Sure some to vex, but never all to please;
'Tis what the vicious fear, the virtuous shun,
By fools 'tis hated, and by knaves undone!
    If wit so much from ignorance undergo,
Ah, let not learning too commence its foe!
Of old, those met rewards who could excel,
And such were praised who but endeavour'd well:
Though triumphs were to generals only due,
Crowns were reserved to grace the soldiers too.
Now, they who reach Parnassus' lofty crown,
Employ their pains to spurn some others down;
And while self-love each jealous writer rules,
Contending wits become the sport of fools:
But still the worst with most regret commend,
For each ill author is as bad a friend.
To what base ends, and by what abject ways,
Are mortals urged through sacred lust of praise!
Ah ne'er so dire a thirst of glory boast,
Nor in the critic let the man be lost.
Good nature and good sense must ever join;
To err is human, to forgive, divine.
    But if in noble minds some dregs remain,
Not yet purged off, of spleen and sour disdain;

Discharge that rage on more provoking crimes,
Nor fear a dearth in these flagitious times.
No pardon vile obscenity should find,
Though wit and art conspire to move your mind;
But dulness with obscenity must prove
As shameful sure as impotence in love.
In the fat age of pleasure, wealth, and ease,
Sprung the rank weed, and thrived with large increase:
When love was all an easy monarch's care;
Seldom at council, never in a war:
Jilts ruled the state, and statesmen farces writ;
Nay wits had pensions, and young lords had wit:
The fair sat panting at a courtier's play,
And not a mask went unimproved away:
The modest fan was lifted up no more,
And virgins smiled at what they blush'd before.
The following licence of a foreign reign
Did all the dregs of bold Socinus drain;
Then unbelieving priests reform'd the nation,
And taught more pleasant methods of salvation;
Where Heaven's free subjects might their rights dispute,
Lest God Himself should seem too absolute:
Pulpits their sacred satire learn'd to spare,
And vice admired to find a flatterer there!
Encouraged thus, Wit's Titans braved the skies,
And the press groan'd with licensed blasphemies.
These monsters, critics! with your darts engage,
Here point your thunder, and exhaust your rage!
Yet shun their fault, who, scandalously nice,
Will needs mistake an author into vice;
All seems infected that th' infected spy,
As all looks yellow to the jaundiced eye.

III

Learn then what morals critics ought to show,
For 'tis but half a judge's task, to know.
'Tis not enough, taste, judgment, learning, join;
In all you speak, let truth and candour shine:
That not alone what to your sense is due
All may allow; but seek your friendship too.
    Be silent always, when you doubt your sense;

And speak, though sure, with seeming diffidence:
Some positive, persisting fops we know,
Who, if once wrong, will needs be always so;
But you, with pleasure own your errors past,
And make each day a critique on the last.
    'Tis not enough your counsel still be true;
Blunt truths more mischief than nice falsehoods do;
Men must be taught as if you taught them not,
And things unknown proposed as things forgot.
Without good-breeding, truth is disapproved;
That only makes superior sense beloved.
    Be niggards of advice on no pretence;
For the worst avarice is that of sense.
With mean complaisance ne'er betray your trust,
Nor be so civil as to prove unjust.
Fear not the anger of the wise to raise;
Those best can bear reproof who merit praise.
    'Twere well might critics still this freedom take,
But Appius[7] reddens at each word you speak,
And stares, tremendous, with a threatening eye,
Like some fierce tyrant in old tapestry.
Fear most to tax an Honourable fool,
Whose right it is, uncensured, to be dull;
Such, without wit, are poets when they please,
As without learning they can take degrees.
Leave dangerous truths to unsuccessful satires,
And flattery to fulsome dedicators,
Whom, when they praise, the world believes no more,
Than when they promise to give scribbling o'er.
'Tis best sometimes your censure to restrain,
And charitably let the dull be vain:
Your silence there is better than your spite,
For who can rail so long as they can write?
Still humming on, their drowsy course they keep,
And lash'd so long, like tops, are lash'd asleep.
False steps but help them to renew the race,
As, after stumbling, jades will mend their pace.
What crowds of these, impenitently bold,
In sounds and jingling syllables grown old,

---

[7] A character in a play by John Dennis.

Still run on poets in a raging vein,
Even to the dregs and squeezings of the brain,
Strain out the last dull dropping of their sense,
And rhyme with all the rage of impotence!
    Such shameless bards we have; and yet 'tis true
There are as mad, abandon'd critics too.
The bookful blockhead, ignorantly read,
With loads of learned lumber in his head,
With his own tongue still edifies his ears,
And always listening to himself appears.
All books he reads, and all he reads assails,
From Dryden's Fables down to D'Urfey's Tales:
With him, most authors steal their works, or buy;
Garth did not write his own Dispensary.
Name a new play, and he's the poet's friend,
Nay show'd his faults — but when would poets mend?
No place so sacred from such fops is barr'd,
Nor is Paul's church more safe than Paul's church-yard:
Nay, fly to altars; there they'll talk you dead;
For fools rush in where angels fear to tread,
Distrustful sense with modest caution speaks,
It still looks home, and short excursions makes;
But rattling nonsense in full volleys breaks,
And never shock'd, and never turn'd aside,
Bursts out, resistless, with a thundering tide.
    But where's the man who counsel can bestow,
Still pleased to teach, and yet not proud to know?
Unbiass'd, or by favour, or by spite;
Not dully prepossess'd, nor blindly right;
Though learn'd, well-bred; and though well-bred,
        sincere;
Modestly bold, and humanly severe:
Who to a friend his faults can freely show,
And gladly praise the merit of a foe?
Bless'd with a taste exact, yet unconfined;
A knowledge both of books and human kind;
Generous converse; a soul exempt from pride;
And love to praise, with reason on his side?
    Such once were critics; such the happy few,
Athens and Rome in better ages knew.
The mighty Stagyrite first left the shore,

Spread all his sails, and durst the deeps explore;
He steer'd securely, and discover'd far,
Led by the light of the Mæonian star.
Poets, a race long unconfined, and free,
Still fond and proud of savage liberty,
Received his laws; and stood convinced 'twas fit,
Who conquer'd Nature, should preside o'er Wit.
  Horace still charms with graceful negligence,
And without method talks us into sense,
Will, like a friend, familiarly convey
The truest notions in the easiest way.
He, who supreme in judgment, as in wit,
Might boldly censure, as he boldly writ,
Yet judged with coolness, though he sung with fire;
His precepts teach but what his works inspire.
Our critics take a contrary extreme,
They judge with fury, but they write with phlegm:
Nor suffers Horace more in wrong translations
By wits, than critics in as wrong quotations.
  See Dionysius Homer's thoughts refine,
And call new beauties forth from every line!
  Fancy and art in gay Petronius please,
The scholar's learning with the courtier's ease.
  In grave Quintilian's copious work, we find
The justest rules and clearest method join'd:
Thus useful arms in magazines we place,
All ranged in order, and disposed with grace,
But less to please the eye, than arm the hand,
Still fit for use, and ready at command.
  Thee, bold Longinus! all the Nine inspire,
And bless their critic with a poet's fire.
An ardent judge, who, zealous in his trust,
With warmth gives sentence, yet is always just:
Whose own example strengthens all his laws:
And is himself that great sublime he draws.
  Thus long succeeding critics justly reign'd,
Licence repress'd, and useful laws ordain'd.
Learning and Rome alike in empire grew;
And arts still follow'd where her eagles flew;
From the same foes, at last, both felt their doom,
And the same age saw Learning fall, and Rome.

With Tyranny, then Superstition join'd,
As that the body, this enslaved the mind;
Much was believed, but little understood,
And to be dull was construed to be good;
A second deluge learning thus o'errun,
And the monks finish'd what the Goths begun.
    At length Erasmus, that great injured name,
(The glory of the priesthood, and the shame!)
Stemm'd the wild torrent of a barbarous age,
And drove those holy Vandals off the stage.
    But see! each Muse, in Leo's golden days,
Starts from her trance, and trims her wither'd bays;
Rome's ancient Genius, o'er its ruins spread,
Shakes off the dust, and rears his reverend head.
Then Sculpture and her sister-arts revive;
Stones leaped to form, and rocks began to live;
With sweeter notes each rising temple rung;
A Raphael painted, and a Vida sung.
Immortal Vida: on whose honour'd brow
The poet's bays and critic's ivy grow:
Cremona now shall ever boast thy name,
As next in place to Mantua, next in fame!
    But soon by impious arms from Latium chased,
Their ancient bounds the banish'd Muses pass'd;
Thence Arts o'er all the northern world advance,
But critic-learning flourish'd most in France;
The rules a nation, born to serve, obeys;
And Boileau still in right of Horace sways.
But we, brave Britons, foreign laws despised,
And kept unconquer'd, and uncivilised;
Fierce for the liberties of wit and bold,
We still defied the Romans, as of old.
Yet some there were, among the sounder few
Of those who less presumed, and better knew,
Who durst assert the juster ancient cause,
And here restored Wit's fundamental laws.
Such was the Muse, whose rules and practice tell,
"Nature's chief Masterpiece is writing well,"[8]

---

[8] From the *Essay on Poetry* by the Duke of Buckingham.

Such was Roscommon, not more learn'd than good,
With manners generous as his noble blood;
To him the wit of Greece and Rome was known,
And every author's merit, but his own.
Such late was Walsh — the Muse's judge and friend,
Who justly knew to blame or to commend:
To failings mild, but zealous for desert;
The clearest head, and the sincerest heart.
This humble praise, lamented shade! receive,
This praise at least a grateful Muse may give:
The Muse, whose early voice you taught to sing,
Prescribed her heights, and pruned her tender wing,
(Her guide now lost) no more attempts to rise,
But in low numbers short excursions tries:
Content, if hence the unlearn'd their wants may view,
The learn'd reflect on what before they knew;
Careless of censure, nor too fond of fame;
Still pleased to praise, yet not afraid to blame;
Averse alike to flatter, or offend;
Not free from faults, nor yet too vain to mend.

The Rape of the Lock

Dedication to Mrs. Arabella Fermor

MADAM, — It will be in vain to deny that I have some regard for this piece, since I dedicate it to you. Yet you may bear me witness, it was intended only to divert a few young ladies, who have good sense and good humour enough to laugh not only at their sex's little unguarded follies, but at their own. But as it was communicated with the air of a secret, it soon found its way into the world. An imperfect copy having been offered to a bookseller, you had the good-nature for my sake to consent to the publication of one more correct: this I was forced to before I had executed half my design, for the machinery was entirely wanting to complete it.

The machinery, Madam, is a term invented by the critics to signify that part which the Deities, Angels, or Dæmons are made to act in a Poem: for the ancient Poets are in one respect like many modern ladies: let an action be never so trivial in itself, they always make it appear of the utmost importance. These machines I determined to raise on a very new and odd foundation, the Rosicrucian doctrine of Spirits.

I know how disagreeable it is to make use of hard words before a lady; but 'tis so much the concern of a Poet to have his works understood, and particularly by your sex, that you must give me leave to explain two or three difficult terms.

The Rosicrucians are a people I must bring you acquainted with. The best account I know of them is in a French book called *Le Comte de Gabalis*, which, both in its title and size, is so like a novel that many of the fair sex have read it for one by mistake. According to these gentlemen, the four elements are inhabited by Spirits which they call Sylphs, Gnomes, Nymphs and Salamanders. The Gnomes, or Dæmons of Earth, delight in mischief; but the Sylphs, whose habitation is in the air, are the best-conditioned creatures imaginable. For they say any mortals may enjoy the most intimate familiarities with these gentle Spirits, upon a condition very easy to all true adepts, an inviolate preservation of chastity.

As to the following Cantos, all the passages of them are as fabulous as the vision at the beginning, or the transformation at the end (except the loss of your hair, which I always mention with reverence). The human persons are as fictitious as the airy ones; and the character of Belinda, as it is now managed, resembles you in nothing but in beauty.

If this Poem had as many graces as there are in your person, or in your mind, yet I could never hope it should pass through the world half so uncensured as you have done. But let its fortune be what it will, mine is happy enough, to have given me this occasion of assuring you that I am, with the truest esteem, Madam, your most obedient, humble Servant,

A. POPE.

Nolueram, Belinda, tuos violare capillos;
Sed juvat, hoc precibus me tribuisse tuis. — MART.[9]

CANTO I

What dire offence from amorous causes springs,
What mighty contests rise from trivial things,
I sing—This verse to CARYLL,[10] Muse! is due:
This, even Belinda may vouchsafe to view;
Slight is the subject, but not so the praise,
If she inspire, and he approve my lays.

   Say what strange motive, goddess! could compel
A well-bred lord to assault a gentle belle?
O say what stranger cause, yet unexplored,

---

[9] "I had not wished to violate your hair, Belinda, but it is pleasing for me to attribute this to your prayers." — Martial.

[10] John Caryll, a friend with whom Pope maintained a long correspondence.

Could make a gentle belle reject a lord?
In tasks so bold, can little men engage,
And in soft bosoms dwells such mighty rage?
　　Sol through white curtains shot a tim'rous ray,
And oped those eyes that must eclipse the day:
Now lap-dogs give themselves the rousing shake,
And sleepless lovers, just at twelve awake:
Thrice rung the bell, the slipper knock'd the ground,
And the press'd watch return'd a silver sound.
Belinda still her downy pillow press'd,
Her guardian sylph prolong'd the balmy rest:
'Twas he had summon'd to her silent bed
The morning-dream that hover'd o'er her head?
A youth more glittering than a birth-night beau,
(That ev'n in slumber caused her cheek to glow)
Seem'd to her ear his winning lips to lay,
And thus in whispers said, or seem'd to say:
　　"Fairest of mortals, thou distinguish'd care
Of thousand bright inhabitants of air!
If e'er one vision touch'd thy infant thought,
Of all the nurse and all the priest have taught;
Of airy elves by moonlight shadows seen,
The silver token, and the circled green,
Or virgins visited by angel powers,
With golden crowns and wreaths of heavenly flowers;
Hear and believe! thy own importance know,
Nor bound thy narrow views to things below.
Some secret truths, from learned pride conceal'd,
To maids alone and children are reveal'd:
What though no credit doubting wits may give?
The fair and innocent shall still believe.
Know, then, unnumbered spirits round thee fly,
The light militia of the lower sky:
These, though unseen, are ever on the wing,
Hang o'er the box, and hover round the ring.
Think what an equipage thou hast in air,
And view with scorn two pages and a chair.
As now your own, our beings were of old;
And once inclosed in woman's beauteous mould;
Thence, by a soft transition, we repair
From earthly vehicles to these of air.

Think not, when woman's transient breath is fled,
That all her vanities at once are dead;
Succeeding vanities she still regards,
And though she plays no more, o'erlooks the cards.
Her joy in gilden chariots, when alive,
And love of ombre, after death survive.
For when the fair in all their pride expire,
To their first elements their souls retire:
The sprites of fiery termagants in flame
Mount up, and take a Salamander's name.
Soft yielding minds to water glide away,
And sip, with nymphs, their elemental tea.
The graver prude sinks downward to a gnome,
In search of mischief still on earth to roam.
The light coquettes in sylphs aloft repair,
And sport and flutter in the fields of air.
    "Know further yet; whoever fair and chaste
Rejects mankind, is by some sylph embraced:
For spirits, freed from mortal laws, with ease
Assume what sexes and what shapes they please.
What guards the purity of melting maids,
In courtly balls, and midnight masquerades,
Safe from the treach'rous friend, the daring spark,
The glance by day, the whisper in the dark,
When kind occasion prompts their warm desires,
When music softens, and when dancing fires?
'Tis but their sylph, the wise celestials know,
Though honour is the word with men below.
    "Some nymphs there are, too conscious of their face,
For life predestined to the gnomes embrace.
These swell their prospects and exalt their pride,
When offers are disdain'd and love denied:
Then gay ideas crowd the vacant brain,
While peers, and dukes, and all their sweeping train,
And garters, stars, and coronets appear,
And in soft sounds, 'Your Grace' salutes their ear.
'Tis these that early taint the female soul,
Instruct the eyes of young coquettes to roll,
Teach infant cheeks a bidden blush to know,
And little hearts to flutter at a beau.
    "Oft when the world imagine women stray,

The sylphs through mystic mazes guide their way,
Through all the giddy circle they pursue,
And old impertinence expel by new.
What tender maid but must a victim fall
To one man's treat, but for another's ball?
When Florio speaks, what virgin could withstand,
If gentle Damon did not squeeze her hand?
With varying vanities, from ev'ry part,
They shift the moving toy-shop of their heart;
Where wigs with wigs, with sword-knots sword-knots strive,
Beaux banish beaux, and coaches coaches drive.
This erring mortals levity may call,
Oh, blind to truth! the sylphs contrive it all.
      "Of these am I, who thy protection claim,
A watchful sprite, and Ariel is my name.
Late, as I ranged the crystal wilds of air,
In the clear mirror of thy ruling star
I saw, alas! some dread event impend,
Ere to the main this morning sun descend;
But heaven reveals not what, or how, or where:
Warn'd by the sylph, oh, pious maid, beware!
This to disclose is all thy guardian can:
Beware of all, but most beware of man!"
      He said; when Shock, who thought she slept too long,
Leap'd up, and waked his mistress with his tongue.
'Twas then, Belinda, if report say true,
Thy eyes first open'd on a billet-doux;
Wounds, charms, and ardours, were no sooner read,
But all the vision vanish'd from thy head.
      And now, unveil'd, the toilet stands display'd,
Each silver vase in mystic order laid.
First, robed in white, the nymph intent adores,
With head uncover'd, the cosmetic powers.
A heav'nly image in the glass appears,
To that she bends, to that her eye she rears;
Th' inferior priestess, at her altar's side,
Trembling, begins the sacred rites of pride.
Unnumber'd treasures ope at once, and here
The various offerings of the world appear;
From each she nicely culls with curious toil,
And decks the goddess with the glitt'ring spoil.

This casket India's glowing gems unlocks,
And all Arabia breathes from yonder box.
The tortoise here and elephant unite,
Transform'd to combs, the speckled and the white.
Here files of pins extend their shining rows,
Puffs, powders, patches, Bibles, billet-doux.
Now awful beauty puts on all its arms;
The fair each moment rises in her charms,
Repairs her smiles, awakens every grace,
And calls forth all the wonders of her face:
Sees by degrees a purer blush arise,
And keener lightnings quicken in her eyes.
The busy sylphs surround their darling care,
These set the head, and those divide the hair,
Some fold the sleeve, while others plait the gown;
And Betty's praised for labours not her own.

CANTO II

Not with more glories, in th' ethereal plain,
The sun first rises o'er the purpled main,
Than, issuing forth, the rival of his beams
Launch'd on the bosom of the silver Thames.
Fair nymphs and well-dress'd youths around her shone,
But every eye was fix'd on her alone.
On her white breast a sparkling cross she wore,
Which Jews might kiss, and infidels adore.
Her lively looks a sprightly mind disclose,
Quick as her eyes, and as unfix'd as those:
Favours to none, to all she smiles extends;
Oft she rejects, but never once offends.
Bright as the sun, her eyes the gazers strike,
And, like the sun, they shine on all alike.
Yet graceful ease, and sweetness void of pride,
Might hide her faults, if belles had faults to hide:
If to her share some female errors fall,
Look on her face, and you'll forget them all.
    This nymph, to the destruction of mankind,
Nourish'd two locks, which graceful hung behind
In equal curls, and well conspired to deck
With shining ringlets the smooth ivory neck.

Love in these labyrinths his slaves detains,
And mighty hearts are held in slender chains.
With hairy springes we the birds betray,
Slight lines of hair surprise the finny prey,
Fair tresses man's imperial race insnare,
And beauty draws us with a single hair.

Th' adventurous baron the bright locks admired;
He saw, he wish'd, and to the prize aspired.
Resolved to win, he meditates the way,
By force to ravish, or by fraud betray;
For when success a lover's toils attends,
Few ask, if fraud or force attain'd his ends.

For this, ere Phœbus rose, he had implored
Propitious Heaven, and every power adored:
But chiefly Love — to Love an altar built,
Of twelve vast French romances, neatly gilt.
There lay three garters, half a pair of gloves;
And all the trophies of his former loves:
With tender billet-doux he lights the pyre,
And breathes three amorous sighs to raise the fire.
Then prostrate falls, and begs with ardent eyes
Soon to obtain, and long possess the prize:
The powers gave ear, and granted half his prayer,
The rest, the winds dispersed in empty air.

But now secure the painted vessel glides,
The sun-beams trembling on the floating tides;
While melting music steals upon the sky,
And soften'd sounds along the waters die;
Smooth flow the waves, the zephyrs gently play,
Belinda smiled, and all the world was gay.
All but the sylph — with careful thoughts oppress'd,
Th' impending woe sat heavy on his breast.
He summons straight his denizens of air;
The lucid squadrons round the sails repair:
Soft o'er the shrouds aërial whispers breathe,
That seem'd but zephyrs to the train beneath.
Some to the sun their insect-wings unfold,
Waft on the breeze, or sink in clouds of gold;
Transparent forms, too fine for mortal sight,
Their fluid bodies half dissolved in light.
Loose to the wind their airy garments flew,

Thin glittering textures of the filmy dew,
Dipp'd in the richest tincture of the skies,
Where light disports in ever-mingling dyes;
While ev'ry beam new transient colours flings,
Colours that change whene'er they wave their wings.
Amid the circle on the gilded mast,
Superior by the head, was Ariel placed;
His purple pinions op'ning to the sun,
He raised his azure wand, and thus begun:
    "Ye sylphs and sylphids, to your chief give ear;
Fays, fairies, genii, elves, and dæmons, hear:
Ye know the spheres, and various tasks assign'd
By laws eternal to the aërial kind.
Some in the fields of purest ether play,
And bask and whiten in the blaze of day.
Some guide the course of wand'ring orbs on high,
Or roll the planets through the boundless sky.
Some less refined beneath the moon's pale light
Pursue the stars that shoot athwart the night,
Or suck the mists in grosser air below,
Or dip their pinions in the painted bow,
Or brew fierce tempests on the wintry main,
Or o'er the glebe distil the kindly rain.
Others on earth o'er human race preside,
Watch all their ways, and all their actions guide:
Of these the chief the care of nations own,
And guard with arms divine the British throne.
    "Our humbler province is to tend the fair,
Not a less pleasing, though less glorious care;
To save the powder from too rude a gale,
Nor let the imprison'd essences exhale;
To draw fresh colours from the vernal flowers;
To steal from rainbows, ere they drop in showers,
A brighter wash; to curl their waving hairs,
Assist their blushes and inspire their airs;
Nay, oft, in dreams, invention we bestow,
To change a flounce, or add a furbelow.
    "This day, black omens threat the brightest fair
That e'er deserved a watchful spirit's care;
Some dire disaster, or by force, or flight;
But what, or where, the Fates have wrapp'd in night.

Whether the nymph shall break Diana's law,
Or some frail china-jar receive a flaw;
Or stain her honour or her new brocade;
Forget her prayers, or miss a masquerade;
Or lose her heart, or necklace, at a ball;
Or whether Heaven has doom'd that Shock must fall.
Haste, then, ye spirits! to your charge repair:
The flutt'ring fan be Zephyretta's care;
The drops to thee, Brillante, we consign;
And, Momentilla, let the watch be thine;
Do thou, Crispissa, tend her fav'rite lock;
Ariel himself shall be the guard of Shock.
"To fifty chosen sylphs, of special note,
We trust th' important charge, the petticoat:
Oft have we known that seven-fold fence to fail,
Though stiff with hoops, and arm'd with ribs of whale;
Form a strong line about the silver bound,
And guard the wide circumference around.
"Whatever spirit, careless of his charge,
His post neglects, or leaves the fair at large,
Shall feel sharp vengeance soon o'ertake his sins,
Be stopp'd in vials, or transfix'd with pins;
Or plunged in lakes of bitter washes lie,
Or wedged whole ages in a bodkin's eye:
Gums and pomatums shall his flight restrain,
While clogg'd he beats his silken wings in vain:
Or alum styptics with contracting power
Shrink his thin essence like a rivell'd flower:
Or, as Ixion fix'd, the wretch shall feel
The giddy motion of the whirling wheel,
In fumes of burning chocolate shall glow,
And tremble at the sea that froths below!"
He spoke; the spirits from the sails descend;
Some, orb in orb, around the nymph extend;
Some thrid the mazy ringlets of her hair;
Some hang upon the pendants of her ear:
With beating hearts the dire event they wait,
Anxious and trembling for the birth of Fate.

CANTO III

Close by those meads, for ever crown'd with flowers,
Where Thames with pride surveys his rising towers,
There stands a structure of majestic frame,
Which from the neighb'ring Hampton takes its name.
Here Britain's statesmen oft the fall foredoom
Of foreign tyrants, and of nymphs at home;
Here thou, great ANNA! whom three realms obey,
Dost sometimes counsel take — and sometimes tea.
    Hither the heroes and the nymphs resort,
To taste a while the pleasures of a court;
In various talk th' instructive hours they pass'd,
Who gave the ball, or paid the visit last;
One speaks the glory of the British Queen,
And one describes a charming Indian screen;
A third interprets motions, looks, and eyes;
At every word a reputation dies.
Snuff, or the fan, supply each pause of chat,
With singing, laughing, ogling, *and all that*.
    Meanwhile, declining from the noon of day,
The sun obliquely shoots his burning ray;
The hungry judges soon the sentence sign,
And wretches hang that jurymen may dine;
The merchant from th' exchange returns in peace,
And the long labours of the toilet cease.
Belinda now, whom thirst of fame invites,
Burns to encounter two adventurous knights,
At ombre singly to decide their doom;
And swells her breast with conquests yet to come.
Straight the three bands prepare in arms to join,
Each band the number of the sacred nine.
Soon as she spreads her hand, th' aërial guard
Descend, and sit on each important card:
First Ariel perch'd upon a Matadore,
Then each according to the rank he bore;
For sylphs, yet mindful of their ancient race,
Are, as when women, wondrous fond of place.
    Behold, four Kings in majesty revered,
With hoary whiskers and a forky beard;
And four fair Queens, whose hands sustain a flower,

Th' expressive emblem of their softer power;
Four knaves in garbs succinct, a trusty band;
Caps on their heads, and halberts in their hand;
And party-colour'd troops, a shining train,
Drawn forth to combat on the velvet plain.
    The skilful nymph reviews her force with care:
"Let Spades be trumps!" she said, and trumps they were.
    Now move to war her sable Matadores,
In show like leaders of the swarthy Moors.
Spadillio first, unconquerable lord!
Led off two captive trumps, and swept the board.
As many more Manillio forced to yield,
And march'd a victor from the verdant field.
Him Basto follow'd; but his fate more hard
Gain'd but one trump, and one plebeian card.
With his broad sabre next, a chief in years,
The hoary Majesty of Spades appears,
Puts forth one manly leg, to sight reveal'd,
The rest, his many-colour'd robe conceal'd.
The rebel Knave, who dares his prince engage,
Proves the just victim of his royal rage.
Ev'n mighty Pam, that kings and queens o'erthrew,
And mow'd down armies in the fights of Lu,
Sad chance of war! now destitute of aid,
Falls undistinguish'd by the victor Spade!
    Thus far both armies to Belinda yield;
Now to the baron fate inclines the field.
His warlike Amazon her host invades,
Th' imperial consort of the crown of Spades.
The Club's black tyrant first her victim dyed,
Spite of his haughty mien, and barb'rous pride:
What boots the regal circle on his head,
His giant limbs, in state unwieldy spread;
That long behind he trails his pompous robe,
And, of all monarchs, only grasps the globe?
    The baron now his Diamonds pours apace;
Th' embroider'd King who shows but half his face,
And his refulgent Queen, with powers combined
Of broken troops an easy conquest find.
Clubs, Diamonds, Hearts, in wild disorder seen,
With throngs promiscuous strow the level green.

Thus when dispersed a routed army runs,
Of Asia's troops, and Afric's sable sons,
With like confusion different nations fly,
Of various habit, and of various dye,
The pierced battalions disunited fall,
In heaps on heaps; one fate o'erwhelms them all.
   The Knave of Diamonds tries his wily arts,
And wins (oh shameful chance!) the Queen of Hearts.
At this, the blood the virgin's cheek forsook,
A livid paleness spreads o'er all her look;
She sees, and trembles at th' approaching ill,
Just in the jaws of ruin, and Codille.[11]
And now (as oft in some distemper'd state)
On one nice trick depends the gen'ral fate,
An Ace of Hearts steps forth: the King unseen
Lurk'd in her hand, and mourn'd his captive Queen:
He springs to vengeance with an eager pace,
And falls like thunder on the prostrate Ace.
The nymph exulting fills with shouts the sky;
The walls, the woods, and long canals reply.
   O thoughtless mortals! ever blind to fate,
Too soon dejected, and too soon elate.
Sudden, these honours shall be snatch'd away,
And cursed for ever this victorious day.
   For lo! the board with cups and spoons is crown'd,
The berries crackle, and the mill turns round:
On shining altars of Japan they raise
The silver lamp; the fiery spirits blaze:
From silver spouts the grateful liquors glide,
While China's earth receives the smoking tide:
At once they gratify their scent and taste,
And frequent cups prolong the rich repast.
Straight hover round the fair her airy band;
Some, as she sipp'd, the fuming liquor fann'd,
Some o'er her lap their careful plumes display'd,
Trembling, and conscious of the rich brocade.
Coffee (which makes the politician wise,
And see through all things with his half-shut eyes)

---

[11] Loss of the game.

Sent up in vapours to the baron's brain
New stratagems, the radiant lock to gain.
Ah cease, rash youth! desist ere 'tis too late,
Fear the just gods, and think of Scylla's fate!
Changed to a bird, and sent to flit in air,
She dearly pays for Nisus' injured hair!
    But when to mischief mortals bend their will,
How soon they find fit instruments of ill!
Just then, Clarissa drew with tempting grace
A two-edged weapon from her shining case:
So ladies, in romance, assist their knight,
Present the spear, and arm him for the fight.
He takes the gift with reverence and extends
The little engine on his fingers' ends;
This just behind Belinda's neck he spread,
As o'er the fragrant steams she bends her head.
Swift to the lock a thousand sprites repair,
A thousand wings, by turns, blow back the hair;
And thrice they twitch'd the diamond in her ear;
Thrice she look'd back, and thrice the foe drew near.
Just in that instant, anxious Ariel sought
The close recesses of the virgin's thought:
As on the nosegay in her breast reclin'd,
He watch'd th' ideas rising in her mind,
Sudden he view'd, in spite of all her art,
An earthly lover lurking at her heart.
Amazed, confused, he found his power expired,
Resign'd to fate, and with a sigh retired.
The peer now spreads the glitt'ring forfex wide,
T' inclose the lock; now joins it, to divide.
Ev'n then, before the fatal engine closed,
A wretched sylph too fondly interposed;
Fate urged the shears, and cut the sylph in twain,
(But airy substance soon unites again)
The meeting points the sacred hair dissever
From the fair head, for ever, and for ever!
    Then flash'd the living lightning from her eyes,
And screams of horror rend th' affrighted skies.
Not louder shrieks to pitying Heaven are cast,
When husbands or when lap-dogs breathe their last;
Or when rich China vessels, fall'n from high,

In glitt'ring dust and painted fragments lie!
    "Let wreaths of triumph now my temples twine,
(The victor cried) the glorious prize is mine!
While fish in streams, or birds delight in air,
Or in a coach and six the British fair,
As long as *Atalantis*[12] shall be read,
Or the small pillow grace a lady's bed,
While visits shall be paid on solemn days,
When numerous wax-lights in bright order blaze,
While nymphs take treats, or assignations give,
So long my honour, name, and praise shall live!"
What Time would spare, from steel receives its date,
And monuments, like men, submit to fate!
Steel could the labour of the gods destroy,
And strike to dust th' imperial towers of Troy;
Steel could the works of mortal pride confound,
And hew triumphal arches to the ground.
What wonder then, fair nymph! thy hairs should feel
The conquering force of unresisted steel?

CANTO IV

But anxious cares the pensive nymph oppress'd,
And secret passions labour'd in her breast.
Not youthful kings in battle seized alive,
Not scornful virgins who their charms survive,
Not ardent lovers robb'd of all their bliss,
Not ancient ladies when refused a kiss,
Not tyrants fierce that unrepenting die,
Not Cynthia when her manteau's pinn'd awry,
E'er felt such rage, resentment, and despair,
As thou, sad virgin! for thy ravish'd hair.
    For, that sad moment, when the sylphs withdrew,
And Ariel weeping from Belinda flew,
Umbriel, a dusky, melancholy sprite,
As ever sullied the fair face of light,
Down to the central earth, his proper scene,
Repair'd to search the gloomy Cave of Spleen.

---

[12] *The New Atalantis*, a scandalous book by Mary Manley.

Swift on his sooty pinions flits the gnome,
And in a vapour reach'd the dismal dome.
No cheerful breeze this sullen region knows,
The dreaded east is all the wind that blows.
Here in a grotto, shelter'd close from air,
And screen'd in shades from day's detested glare,
She sighs for ever on her pensive bed,
Pain at her side, and Megrim at her head.
Two handmaids wait the throne: alike in place,
But diff'ring far in figure and in face.
Here stood Ill-nature like an ancient maid,
Her wrinkled form in black and white array'd;
With store of prayers, for mornings, nights, and noons,
Her hand is fill'd; her bosom with lampoons.
    There Affectation, with a sickly mien,
Shows in her cheek the roses of eighteen,
Practised to lisp, and hang the head aside,
Faints into airs, and languishes with pride,
On the rich quilt sinks with becoming woe,
Wrapp'd in a gown, for sickness, and for show.
The fair ones feel such maladies as these,
When each new night-dress gives a new disease.
    A constant vapour o'er the palace flies;
Strange phantoms rising as the mists arise;
Dreadful, as hermits' dreams in haunted shades,
Or bright, as visions of expiring maids.
Now glaring fiends, and snakes on rolling spires,
Pale spectres, gaping tombs, and purple fires:
Now lakes of liquid gold, Elysian scenes,
And crystal domes, and angels in machines.
    Unnumber'd throngs on every side are seen
Of bodies changed to various forms by Spleen.
Here living tea-pots stand, one arm held out,
One bent; the handle this, and that the spout:
A pipkin there, like Homer's tripod walks;
Here sighs a jar, and there a goose-pie talks:
Men prove with child, as powerful fancy works,
And maids turn'd bottles call aloud for corks.
    Safe pass'd the gnome through this fantastic band,
A branch of healing spleen-wort in his hand.
Then thus address'd the power: "Hail, wayward Queen!

Who rule the sex to fifty from fifteen;
Parent of vapours, and of female wit,
Who give th' hysteric or poetic fit;
On various tempers act by various ways,
Make some take physic, others scribble plays;
Who cause the proud their visits to delay,
And send the godly in a pet to pray;
A nymph there is, that all thy power disdains,
And thousands more in equal mirth maintains.
But oh! if e'er thy gnome could spoil a grace,
Or raise a pimple on a beauteous face,
Like citron waters matrons' cheeks inflame,
Or change complexions at a losing game;
If e'er with airy horns I planted heads,
Or rumpled petticoats, or tumbled beds,
Or caused suspicion when no soul was rude,
Or discomposed the head-dress of a prude,
Or e'er to costive lap-dog gave disease,
Which not the tears of brightest eyes could ease;
Hear me, and touch Belinda with chagrin,
That single act gives half the world the spleen."
    The Goddess with a discontented air
Seems to reject him, though she grants his prayer.
A wondrous bag with both her hands she binds,
Like that where once Ulysses held the winds;
There she collects the force of female lungs,
Sighs, sobs, and passions, and the war of tongues.
A vial next she fills with fainting fears,
Soft sorrows, melting griefs, and flowing tears.
The gnome rejoicing bears her gifts away,
Spreads his black wings, and slowly mounts to day.
    Sunk in Thalestris' arms the nymph he found,
Her eyes dejected, and her hair unbound.
Full o'er their heads the swelling bag he rent,
And all the furies issued at the vent.
Belinda burns with more than mortal ire,
And fierce Thalestris fans the rising fire;
"O wretched maid!" she spread her hands, and cried,
(While Hampton's echoes, "Wretched maid!" replied)
"Was it for this you took such constant care
The bodkin, comb, and essence to prepare?

For this your locks in paper durance bound?
For this with torturing irons wreathed around?
For this with fillets strain'd your tender head,
And bravely bore the double loads of lead?
Gods! shall the ravisher display your hair,
While the fops envy and the ladies stare?
Honour forbid! at whose unrivall'd shrine
Ease, pleasure, virtue, all our sex resign.
Methinks already I your tears survey,
Already hear the horrid things they say,
Already see you a degraded toast,
And all your honour in a whisper lost!
How shall I then your helpless fame defend?
'Twill then be infamy to seem your friend!
And shall this prize, th' inestimable prize,
Exposed through crystal to the gazing eyes,
And heighten'd by the diamond's circling rays,
On that rapacious hand for ever blaze?
Sooner shall grass in Hyde Park Circus grow,
And wits take lodgings in the sound of Bow;
Sooner let earth, air, sea, to Chaos fall,
Men, monkeys, lap-dogs, parrots, perish all!"
    She said; then raging to Sir Plume repairs,
And bids her beau demand the precious hairs.
(Sir Plume of amber snuff-box justly vain,
And the nice conduct of a clouded cane)
With earnest eyes, and round, unthinking face,
He first the snuff-box open'd, then the case,
And then broke out — "My Lord, why, what the devil!
Z — ds! damn the lock! 'fore Gad, you must be civil!
Plague on't! 'tis past a jest — nay prithee, pox!
Give her the hair" — he spoke, and rapp'd his box.
"It grieves me much (replied the peer again)
Who speaks so well should ever speak in vain,
But by this lock, this sacred lock, I swear,
(Which never more shall join its parted hair;
Which never more its honours shall renew,
Clipp'd from the lovely head where late it grew)
That while my nostrils draw the vital air,
This hand, which won it, shall for ever wear."
He spoke, and speaking, in proud triumph spread

The long-contended honours of her head.
   But Umbriel, hateful gnome! forbears not so;
He breaks the vial whence the sorrows flow.
Then see! the nymph in beauteous grief appears,
Her eyes half-languishing, half-drowned in tears;
On her heaved bosom hung her drooping head,
Which, with a sigh, she raised; and thus she said:
   "For ever cursed be this detested day,
Which snatch'd my best, my fav'rite curl away!
Happy! ay ten times happy had I been,
If Hampton Court these eyes had never seen!
Yet am I not the first mistaken maid,
By love of courts to numerous ills betray'd,
Oh had I rather unadmired remain'd
In some lone isle, or distant northern land;
Where the gilt chariot never marks the way,
Where none learn ombre, none e'er taste bohea!
There kept my charms conceal'd from mortal eye,
Like roses that in deserts bloom and die.
What moved my mind with youthful lords to roam?
Oh had I stayed, and said my prayers at home!
'Twas this the morning omens seem'd to tell:
Thrice from my trembling hand the patch-box fell;
The tott'ring china shook without a wind;
Nay, Poll sat mute, and Shock was most unkind!
A sylph too warn'd me of the threats of Fate,
In mystic visions, now believed too late!
See the poor remnants of these slighted hairs!
My hands shall rend what e'en thy rapine spares:
These in two sable ringlets taught to break,
Once gave new beauties to the snowy neck;
The sister-lock now sits uncouth, alone,
And in its fellow's fate foresees its own;
Uncurl'd it hangs, the fatal shears demands,
And tempts, once more, thy sacrilegious hands.
Oh hadst thou, cruel! been content to seize
Hairs less in sight, or any hairs but these!"

CANTO V

She said: the pitying audience melt in tears;
But Fate and Love had stopp'd the baron's ears.
In vain Thalestris with reproach assails,
For who can move when fair Belinda fails?
Not half so fix'd the Trojan could remain,
While Anna begg'd and Dido raged in vain.
Then grave Clarissa graceful waved her fan;
Silence ensued, and thus the nymph began:
  "Say, why are beauties praised and honoured most,
The wise man's passion, and the vain man's toast?
Why deck'd with all that land and sea afford?
Why angels call'd, and angel-like adored?
Why round our coaches crowd the white-glovėd beaux?
Why bows the side-box from its inmost rows?
How vain are all these glories, all our pains,
Unless good sense preserve what beauty gains;
That men may say, when we the front-box grace,
'Behold the first in virtue as in face!'
Oh! if to dance all night, and dress all day,
Charm'd the small-pox, or chased old age away;
Who would not scorn what housewife's cares produce,
Or who would learn one earthly thing of use?
To patch, nay, ogle, might become a saint,
Nor could it sure be such a sin to paint.
But since, alas! frail beauty must decay,
Curl'd or uncurl'd, since locks will turn to grey;
Since painted, or not painted, all shall fade,
And she who scorns a man must die a maid;
What then remains, but well our power to use,
And keep good-humour still, whate'er we lose?
And trust me, dear, good-humour can prevail,
When airs, and flights, and screams, and scolding fail.
Beauties in vain their pretty eyes may roll;
Charms strike the sight, but merit wins the soul."
  So spoke the dame, but no applause ensued;
Belinda frown'd, Thalestris call'd her prude.
"To arms, to arms!" the fierce virago cries,
And swift as lightning to the combat flies.
All side in parties, and begin th' attack:

Fans clap, silks rustle, and tough whalebones crack;
Heroes' and heroines' shouts confusedly rise,
And bass and treble voices strike the skies.
No common weapons in their hands are found,
Like Gods they fight, nor dread a mortal wound.
　　So when bold Homer makes the Gods engage,
And heavenly breasts with human passions rage;
'Gainst Pallas, Mars; Latona, Hermes arms;
And all Olympus rings with loud alarms;
Jove's thunder roars, Heaven trembles all around,
Blue Neptune storms, the bellowing deeps resound:
Earth shakes her nodding towers, the ground gives way,
And the pale ghosts start at the flash of day!
　　Triumphant Umbriel on a sconce's height
Clapp'd his glad wings, and sate to view the fight:
Propp'd on their bodkin spears, the sprites survey
The growing combat, or assist the fray.
　　While through the press enraged Thalestris flies,
And scatters death around from both her eyes,
A beau and witling perish'd in the throng,
One died in metaphor, and one in song.
"O cruel nymph! a living death I bear,"
Cried Dapperwit, and sunk beside his chair.
A mournful glance Sir Fopling upwards cast,
"Those eyes are made so killing," — was his last.
Thus on Mæander's flowery margin lies
Th' expiring swan, and as he sings he dies.
　　When bold Sir Plume had drawn Clarissa down,
Chloe stepp'd in, and kill'd him with a frown;
She smiled to see the doughty hero slain,
But, at her smile, the beau revived again.
　　Now Jove suspends his golden scales in air,
Weighs the men's wits against the lady's hair:
The doubtful beam long nods from side to side;
At length the wits mount up, the hairs subside.
　　See fierce Belinda on the baron flies,
With more than usual lightning in her eyes:
Nor fear'd the chief th' unequal fight to try,
Who sought no more than on his foe to die.
But this bold lord with manly strength endued,
She with one finger and a thumb subdued:

Just where the breath of life his nostrils drew,
A charge of snuff the wily virgin threw;
The gnomes direct, to every atom just,
The pungent grains of titillating dust.
Sudden, with starting tears each eye o'erflows,
And the high dome re-echoes to his nose.
    "Now meet thy fate," incensed Belinda cried,
And drew a deadly bodkin from her side.
(The same, his ancient personage to deck,
Her great-great-grandsire wore about his neck,
In three seal rings; which after, melted down,
Form'd a vast buckle for his widow's gown:
Her infant grandame's whistle next it grew,
The bells she jingled, and the whistle blew;
Then in a bodkin graced her mother's hairs,
Which long she wore, and now Belinda wears.)
    "Boast not my fall, (he cried) insulting foe!
Thou by some other shalt be laid as low.
Nor think, to die dejects my lofty mind:
All that I dread is leaving you behind!
Rather than so, ah let me still survive,
And burn in Cupid's flames — but burn alive."
    "Restore the lock!" she cries; and all around
"Restore the lock!" the vaulted roofs rebound.
Not fierce Othello in so loud a strain
Roar'd for the handkerchief that caused his pain.
But see how oft ambitious aims are cross'd,
And chiefs contend till all the prize is lost!
The lock, obtain'd with guilt, and kept with pain,
In every place is sought, but sought in vain:
With such a prize no mortal must be blest,
So Heaven decrees! with Heaven who can contest?
    Some thought it mounted to the lunar sphere,
Since all things lost on earth are treasured there.
There heroes' wits are kept in pond'rous vases,
And beaux' in snuff-boxes and tweezer-cases.
There broken vows, and death-bed alms are found,
And lovers' hearts with ends of riband bound,
The courtier's promises, and sick man's prayers,
The smiles of harlots, and the tears of heirs,
Cages for gnats, and chains to yoke a flea,

Dried butterflies, and tomes of casuistry.
  But trust the Muse — she saw it upward rise,
Though mark'd by none but quick, poetic eyes:
(So Rome's great founder to the heavens withdrew,
To Proculus alone confess'd in view)
A sudden star it shot through liquid air,
And drew behind a radiant trail of hair.
Not Berenice's lock first rose so bright,
The heavens bespangling with dishevell'd light.
The sylphs behold it kindling as it flies,
And pleased pursue its progress through the skies.
  This the beau-monde shall from the Mall survey,
And hail with music its propitious ray.
This the blest lover shall for Venus take,
And send up vows from Rosamonda's lake.
This Partridge[13] soon shall view in cloudless skies,
When next he looks through Galileo's eyes;
And hence th' egregious wizard shall foredoom
The fate of Louis, and the fall of Rome.
  Then cease, bright nymph! to mourn thy ravish'd hair,
Which adds new glory to the shining sphere!
Not all the tresses that fair head can boast
Shall draw such envy as the lock you lost.
For, after all the murders of your eye,
When, after millions slain, yourself shall die;
When those fair suns shall set, as set they must,
And all those tresses shall be laid in dust;
This lock, the Muse shall consecrate to fame,
And 'midst the stars inscribe Belinda's name.

---

[13] The astrologer John Partridge.

Essay on Man

EPISTLE I

Argument.

OF THE NATURE AND STATE OF MAN WITH RESPECT TO THE UNIVERSE

Of man in the abstract. — I. That we can judge only with regard to our own system, being ignorant of the relation of systems and things, ver. 17, etc. II. That man is not to be deemed imperfect, but a being suited to his place and rank in the creation, agreeable to the general order of things, and conformable to ends and relations to him unknown, ver. 35, etc. III. That it is partly upon his ignorance of future events, and partly upon the hope of a future state, that all his happiness in the present depends, ver. 77, etc. IV. The pride of aiming at more knowledge, and pretending to more perfection, the cause of man's error and misery. The impiety of putting himself in the place of God, and judging of the fitness or unfitness, perfection or imperfection, justice or injustice, of His dispensations, ver. 113, etc. V. The absurdity of conceiting himself the final cause of the creation, or expecting that perfection in the moral world which is not in the natural, ver. 131, etc. VI. The unreasonableness of his complaints against Providence, while on the one hand he demands the perfections of the angels and on the other the bodily qualifications of the brutes; though to possess any of the sensitive faculties in a higher degree would render him miserable, ver. 173, etc. VII. That throughout the whole visible world an universal order and gradation in the sensual and mental faculties is observed, which causes a subordination of creature to creature, and of all creatures to Man. The gradations of sense, instinct, thought, reflection, reason; that reason alone countervails all the other faculties, ver. 207. VIII. How much farther this order and subordination of living creatures may extend above and below us; were any part of which broken, not that part only, but the whole connected creation, must be destroyed, ver. 233. IX. The extravagance, madness, and pride of such a desire, ver. 259. X. The consequence of all the absolute submission due to Providence, both as to our present and future state, ver. 281, etc., to the end.

Awake, my St. John![14] leave all meaner things
To low ambition and the pride of kings.
Let us (since life can little more supply
Than just to look about us, and to die)

---

[14] The statesman Henry Saint-John, Viscount Bolingbroke.

Expatiate free o'er all this scene of man;
A mighty maze! but not without a plan:
A wild, where weeds and flowers promiscuous shoot;
Or garden, tempting with forbidden fruit.
Together let us beat this ample field,
Try what the open, what the covert yield!
The latent tracts, the giddy heights explore
Of all who blindly creep, or sightless soar;
Eye Nature's walks, shoot folly as it flies,
And catch the manners living as they rise:
Laugh where we must, be candid where we can;
But vindicate the ways of God to man.
   I. Say first, of God above, or man below,
What can we reason, but from what we know?
Of man, what see we but his station here,
From which to reason, or to which refer?
Through worlds unnumbered, though the God be known,
'Tis ours to trace Him only in our own.
He, who through vast immensity can pierce,
See worlds on worlds compose one universe,
Observe how system into system runs,
What other planets circle other suns,
What varied being peoples every star,
May tell why Heaven has made us as we are.
But of this frame the bearings and the ties,
The strong connections, nice dependencies,
Gradations just, has thy pervading soul
Look'd through? or can a part contain the whole?
   Is the great chain, that draws all to agree,
And drawn, supports, upheld by God or thee?
   II. Presumptuous man! the reason wouldst thou find,
Why form'd so weak, so little, and so blind?
First, if thou canst, the harder reason guess,
Why form'd no weaker, blinder, and no less?
Ask of thy mother earth, why oaks are made
Taller and stronger than the weeds they shade?
Or ask of yonder argent fields above,
Why Jove's satellites are less than Jove?
   Of systems possible, if 'tis confess'd,
That Wisdom infinite must form the best,
Where all must full, or not coherent be,

And all that rises, rise in due degree;
Then in the scale of reas'ning life, 'tis plain,
There must be, somewhere, such a rank as man:
And all the question (wrangle e'er so long)
Is only this, if God has placed him wrong?

Respecting man, whatever wrong we call,
May, must be right, as relative to all.
In human works, though labour'd on with pain,
A thousand movements scarce one purpose gain;
In God's, one single can its end produce;
Yet serves to second too, some other use.
So man, who here seems principal alone,
Perhaps acts second to some sphere unknown,
Touches some wheel, or verges to some goal;
'Tis but a part we see, and not a whole.

When the proud steed shall know why man restrains
His fiery course, or drives him o'er the plains;
When the dull ox, why now he breaks the clod,
Is now a victim, and now Egypt's god:
Then shall man's pride and dulness comprehend
His actions', passions', being's use and end;
Why doing, suff'ring, check'd, impell'd; and why
This hour a slave, the next a deity.

Then say not man's imperfect, Heaven in fault;
Say rather, man's as perfect as he ought:
His knowledge measured to his state and place;
His time a moment, and a point his space.
If to be perfect in a certain sphere,
What matter, soon or late, or here or there?
The blest to-day is as completely so,
As who began a thousand years ago.

III. Heaven from all creatures hides the book of Fate,
All but the page prescribed, their present state:
From brutes what men, from men what spirits know:
Or who could suffer being here below?
The lamb thy riot dooms to bleed to-day,
Had he thy reason, would he skip and play?
Pleased to the last, he crops the flowery food,
And licks the hand just raised to shed his blood.
Oh blindness to the future! kindly given,
That each may fill the circle mark'd by Heaven:

Who sees with equal eye, as God of all,
A hero perish, or a sparrow fall,
Atoms or systems into ruin hurl'd,
And now a bubble burst, and now a world.
    Hope humbly then; with trembling pinions soar;
Wait the great teacher, Death; and God adore.
What future bliss, He gives not thee to know,
But gives that hope to be thy blessing now.
Hope springs eternal in the human breast:
Man never Is, but always To be blest.
The soul, uneasy, and confined from home,
Rests and expatiates in a life to come.   *naïve*
                                                            nature
    Lo, the poor Indian! whose untutor'd mind
Sees God in clouds, or hears Him in the wind;
His soul, proud Science never taught to stray
Far as the solar-walk, or milky-way;
Yet simple Nature to his hope has given,
Behind the cloud-topp'd hill, and humbler Heaven,
Some safer world in depth of woods embraced,
Some happier island in the watery waste,
Where slaves once more their native land behold,
No fiends torment, no Christians thirst for gold.
? To Be, contents his natural desire,   *noble*
     He asks no angel's wings, no seraph's fire;   *savage*
     But thinks, admitted to that equal sky,
     His faithful dog shall bear him company.
    IV. Go, wiser thou! and in thy scale of sense,
Weigh thy opinion against Providence;
Call imperfection what thou fanciest such,
Say, here He gives too little, there too much:
Destroy all creatures for thy sport or gust,
pride Yet cry, If man's unhappy, God's unjust;
If man alone engross not Heaven's high care,
Alone made perfect here, immortal there:
|| Snatch from His hand the balance and the rod,
Re-judge His justice, be the god of God.
In pride, in reas'ning pride, our error lies;
All quit their sphere, and rush into the skies.
Pride still is aiming at the blest abodes,
Men would be angels, angels would be gods. *Lucifer*
Aspiring to be gods, if angels fell,

Aspiring to be angels, men rebel:
And who but wishes to invert the laws
Of Order, sins against the Eternal Cause.
   V. Ask for what end the Heavenly bodies shine —
Earth for whose use? Pride answers, "'Tis for mine: *Pride's Claim*
For me kind Nature wakes her genial power,
Suckles each herb, and spreads out ev'ry flower;
Annual for me, the grape, the rose renew,
The juice nectareous, and the balmy dew;
For me, the mine a thousand treasures brings;
For me, health gushes from a thousand springs;
Seas roll to waft me, suns to light me rise;
My footstool earth, my canopy the skies."
   But errs not Nature from this gracious end,
From burning suns when livid deaths descend,
When earthquakes swallow, or when tempests sweep
Towns to one grave, whole nations to the deep?
"No, ('tis replied) the first Almighty Cause   *general not particular??*
Acts not by partial, but by gen'ral laws;
The exceptions few: some change since all began:
And what created perfect?" — Why then man?
If the great end be human happiness,   *If —*
Then Nature deviates; and can man do less?
As much that end a constant course requires
Of showers and sunshine, as of man's desires;
As much eternal springs and cloudless skies,   *But they are then heaven's design*
As men for ever temperate, calm, and wise.
If plagues or earthquakes break not Heaven's design,
Why then a Borgia, or a Catiline?
Who knows but He, whose hand the lightning forms,
Who heaves old Ocean, and who wings the storms;
Pours fierce ambition in a Cæsar's mind,
Or turns young Ammon loose to scourge mankind?
From pride, from pride, our very reas'ning springs;
Account for moral as for natural things:
Why charge we Heaven in those, in these acquit?
In both, to reason right, is to submit.
   · Better for us, perhaps, it might appear,
Were there all harmony, all virtue here;
That never air or ocean felt the wind,
That never passion discomposed the mind.

But all subsists by elemental strife;
And passions are the elements of life.
The general order, since the whole began,
Is kept by Nature, and is kept in man.
   VI. What would this man? Now upward will he soar,
And little less than angel, would be more;
Now looking downwards, just as grieved appears,
To want the strength of bulls, the fur of bears.
Made for his use all creatures if he call,
Say what their use, had he the powers of all?
Nature to these, without profusion, kind,
The proper organs, proper powers assign'd;
Each seeming want compensated of course,
Here with degrees of swiftness, there of force;
All in exact proportion to the state;
Nothing to add, and nothing to abate.
Each beast, each insect, happy in its own:
Is Heaven unkind to man, and man alone?
Shall he alone, whom rational we call,
Be pleased with nothing, if not blest with all?
   The bliss of man (could pride that blessing find)
Is not to act or think beyond mankind;
No powers of body or of soul to share,
But what his Nature and his state can bear.
Why has not man a microscopic eye?
For this plain reason, man is not a fly.
Say what the use, were finer optics given,
To inspect a mite, not comprehend the heaven?
Or touch, if trembling alive all o'er,
To smart and agonise at every pore?
Or quick effluvia darting through the brain,
Die of a rose in aromatic pain?
If Nature thunder'd in his opening ears,
And stunn'd him with the music of the spheres,
How would he wish that Heaven had left him still
The whisp'ring zephyr, and the purling rill?
Who finds not Providence all good and wise,
Alike in what it gives and what denies?
   VII. Far as creation's ample range extends,
The scale of sensual, mental powers ascends:
Mark how it mounts to man's imperial race,

From the green myriads in the peopled grass:
What modes of sight betwixt each wide extreme,   *Sense*
The mole's dim curtain, and the lynx's beam:
Of smell, the headlong lioness between,
And hound sagacious on the tainted green:
Of hearing, from the life that fills the flood,
To that which warbles through the vernal wood?
The spider's touch, how exquisitely fine!
Feels at each thread, and lives along the line:
In the nice bee, what sense so subtly true
From poisonous herbs extract the healing dew?   *instinct*
How instinct varies in the grov'ling swine,
Compared, half-reasoning elephant, with thine!
'Twixt that, and reason, what a nice barrier?
For ever separate, yet for ever near!   ~~Reason~~
Remembrance and reflection, how allied;
What thin partitions sense from thought divide;   *(Reflection)*
And middle natures, how they long to join,   *memory*
Yet never pass the insuperable line!
Without this just gradation could they be
Subjected, these to those, or all to thee?
The powers of all subdued by thee alone,   *Reason*
Is not thy reason all these powers in one?
    VIII. See, through this air, this ocean, and this earth,
All matter quick, and bursting into birth.
Above, how high, progressive life may go!
Around, how wide! how deep extend below!
Vast chain of being! which from God began,
Natures ethereal, human, angel, man,
Beast, bird, fish, insect, what no eye can see,
No glass can reach; from infinite to thee,
From thee to nothing. — On superior powers
Were we to press, inferior might on ours;
Or in the full creation leave a void,
Where, one step broken, the great scale's destroy'd:
From Nature's chain whatever link you strike,
Tenth, or ten thousandth, breaks the chain alike.
    And, if each system in gradation roll
Alike essential to the amazing whole,
The least confusion but in one, not all
That system only, but the whole must fall.

Let earth, unbalanced, from her orbit fly,
Planets and suns run lawless through the sky;
Let ruling angels from their spheres be hurl'd,
Being on being wreck'd, and world on world;
Heaven's whole foundations to their centre nod,
And Nature tremble to the throne of God.
All this dread order break — for whom? for thee?
Vile worm! — oh madness! pride! impiety!

    IX. What if the foot, ordain'd the dust to tread,   *Coriolanus*
Or hand, to toil, aspired to be the head?
What if the head, the eye, or ear repined
To serve mere engines to the ruling mind?
Just as absurd for any part to claim
To be another, in this general frame;
Just as absurd, to mourn the tasks or pains
The great Directing Mind of all ordains.

    All are but parts of one stupendous whole,
Whose body Nature is, and God the soul;
That, changed through all, and yet in all the same;
Great in the earth, as in the ethereal frame;
Warms in the sun, refreshes in the breeze,
Glows in the stars, and blossoms in the trees;
Lives through all life, extends through all extent;
Spreads undivided, operates unspent!
Breathes in our soul, informs our mortal part,   *then can there be*
As full, as perfect, in a hair as heart;   *damnation?*
As full, as perfect in vile man that mourns,
As the rapt seraph that adores and burns:
To him no high, no low, no great, no small;
He fills, He bounds, connects, and equals all.

    X. Cease then, nor order imperfection name:
Our proper bliss depends on what we blame.
Know thy own point: this kind, this due degree
Of blindness, weakness, Heaven bestows on thee.
Submit, in this, or any other sphere,
Secure to be as blest as thou canst bear:
Safe in the hand of one Disposing Power,
Or in the natal, or the mortal hour.
All Nature is but art, unknown to thee   *Nature & chance*
All chance, direction, which thou canst not see;   *are not random*
All discord, harmony not understood;

All partial evil, universal good:
And, spite of pride, in erring reason's spite,
One truth is clear, Whatever is, is right.

EPISTLE II

Argument

OF THE NATURE AND STATE OF MAN WITH RESPECT TO HIMSELF AS AN
INDIVIDUAL

I. The business of Man not to pry into God, but to study himself. His middle
nature: his powers and frailties, ver. 1 to 19. The limits of his capacity, ver. 19,
etc. II. The two principles of man, self-love and reason, both necessary, ver. 53,
etc. Self-love the stronger, and why, ver. 67, etc. Their end the same, ver. 81, etc.
III. The passions, and their use, ver. 93 to 130. The predominant passion, and its
force, ver. 132 to 160. Its necessity in directing men to different purposes, ver.
165, etc. Its providential use, in fixing our principle and ascertaining our virtue,
ver. 177. IV. Virtue and vice joined in our mixed nature; the limits near, yet the
things separate and evident: what is the office of reason, ver. 202 to 216. V. How
odious vice in itself, and how we deceive ourselves into it, ver. 217. VI. That,
however, the ends of Providence and general good are answered in our passions
and imperfections, ver. 238, etc. How usefully these are distributed to all orders
of men, ver. 241. How useful they are to society, ver. 251. And to individuals, ver.
263. In every state, and every age of life, ver. 273, etc.

Know then thyself, presume not God to scan,
The proper study of mankind is man.
Placed on this isthmus of a middle state,
A being darkly wise, and rudely great:
With too much knowledge for the sceptic side,
With too much weakness for the stoic's pride,
He hangs between; in doubt to act, or rest;
In doubt to deem himself a god, or beast;
In doubt his mind or body to prefer;
Born but to die, and reasoning but to err;
Alike in ignorance, his reason such,
Whether he thinks too little, or too much:
Chaos of Thought and Passion, all confused;
Still by himself abused or disabused;
Created half to rise, and half to fall;
Great lord of all things, yet a prey to all;
Sole judge of truth, in endless error hurl'd:

ek lines

The glory, jest, and riddle of the world!
  Go, wondrous creature! mount where Science guides,
Go, measure earth, weigh air, and state the tides;
Instruct the planets in what orbs to run,
Correct old Time, and regulate the sun;
Go, soar with Plato to th' empyreal sphere,
To the first good, first perfect, and first fair;
Or tread the mazy round his followers trod,
And quitting sense call imitating God;
As Eastern priests in giddy circles run,
And turn their heads to imitate the sun.
Go, teach Eternal Wisdom how to rule —
Then drop into thyself, and be a fool!
  Superior beings, when of late they saw
A mortal man unfold all Nature's law,
Admired such wisdom in an earthly shape,
And show'd a Newton as we show an ape.
  Could he, whose rules the rapid comet bind,
Describe or fix one movement of his mind?
Who saw its fires here rise, and there descend,
Explain his own beginning, or his end?
Alas what wonder! Man's superior part
Uncheck'd may rise, and climb from art to art;
But when his own great work is but begun,
What reason weaves, by passion is undone.
  Trace Science then, with modesty thy guide;
First strip off all her equipage of pride;
Deduct but what is vanity or dress,
Or learning's luxury, or idleness;
Or tricks to show the stretch of human brain,
Mere curious pleasure, or ingenious pain;
Expunge the whole, or lop the excrescent parts
Of all our vices have created arts;
Then see how little the remaining sum,
Which served the past, and must the times to come!
  II. Two principles in human nature reign;
Self-love, to urge, and Reason, to restrain;
Nor this a good, nor that a bad we call,
Each works its end, to move or govern all:
And to their proper operation still,
Ascribe all good; to their improper, ill.

Self-love, the spring of motion, acts the soul;
Reason's comparing balance rules the whole.
Man, but for that, no action could attend,
And, but for this, were active to no end:
Fix'd like a plant on his peculiar spot,
To draw nutrition, propagate, and rot:
Or, meteor-like, flame lawless through the void,
Destroying others, by himself destroy'd.
Most strength the moving principle requires;
Active its task, it prompts, impels, inspires.
Sedate and quiet the comparing lies,
Form'd but to check, deliberate, and advise.
Self-love, still stronger, as its objects nigh;
Reason's at distance, and in prospect lie:
That sees immediate good by present sense;
Reason, the future and the consequence.
Thicker than arguments, temptations throng,
At best more watchful this, but that more strong.
The action of the stronger to suspend
Reason still use, to reason still attend.
Attention, habit, and experience gains;
Each strengthens reason, and self-love restrains.
Let subtle schoolmen teach these friends to fight,
More studious to divide than to unite;
And grace and virtue, sense and reason split,
With all the rash dexterity of wit.
Wits, just like fools, at war about a name,
Have full as oft no meaning, or the same.
Self-love and reason to one end aspire,
Pain their aversion, pleasure their desire;
But greedy that its object would devour,
This taste the honey, and not wound the flower:
Pleasure, or wrong or rightly understood,
Our greatest evil, or our greatest good.
    III. Modes of self-love the passions we may call:
'Tis real good, or seeming, moves them all:
But since not every good we can divide,
And reason bids us for our own provide;
Passions, though selfish, if their means be fair,
'List under reason, and deserve her care:
Those that imparted court a nobler aim,

Exalt their kind, and take some virtue's name.
   In lazy apathy let Stoics boast
Their virtue fix'd; 'tis fix'd as in a frost;
Contracted all, retiring to the breast;
But strength of mind is exercise, not rest:
The rising tempest puts in act the soul,
Parts it may ravage, but preserves the whole.
On life's vast ocean diversely we sail,
Reason the card, but passion is the gale;
Nor God alone in the still calm we find,
He mounts the storm, and walks upon the wind.
   Passions, like elements, though born to fight,
Yet, mix'd and soften'd, in His work unite:
These 'tis enough to temper and employ;
But what composes man, can man destroy?
Suffice that reason keep to Nature's road,
Subject, compound them, follow her and God.
Love, hope, and joy, fair pleasure's smiling train,
Hate, fear, and grief, the family of pain,
These mix'd with art, and to due bounds confined,
Make and maintain the balance of the mind:
The lights and shades, whose well-accorded strife
Gives all the strength and colour of our life.
   Pleasures are ever in our hands or eyes;
And when in act, they cease; in prospect, rise:
Present to grasp, and future still to find,
The whole employ of body and of mind.
All spread their charms, but charm not all alike;
On different senses, different objects strike;
Hence different passions more or less inflame,
As strong or weak, the organs of the frame;
And hence one master passion in the breast,
Like Aaron's serpent, swallows up the rest.
   As man, perhaps, the moment of his breath
Receives the lurking principle of death;
The young disease, that must subdue at length,
Grows with his growth, and strengthens with his strength;
So, cast and mingled with his very frame,
The mind's disease, its ruling passion came;
Each vital humour which should feed the whole,
Soon flows to this, in body and in soul:

Whatever warms the heart, or fills the head,
As the mind opens, and its functions spread,
Imagination plies her dangerous art,
And pours it all upon the peccant part.
Nature its mother, habit is its nurse;
Wit, spirit, faculties, but make it worse;
Reason itself but gives it edge and power;
As Heaven's blest beam turns vinegar more sour.
We, wretched subjects though to lawful sway,
In this weak queen some favourite still obey:
Ah! if she lend not arms as well as rules,
What can she more than tell us we are fools?
Teach us to mourn our nature, not to mend,
A sharp accuser, but a helpless friend!
Or from a judge turn pleader, to persuade
The choice we make, or justify it made;
Proud of an easy conquest all along,
She but removes weak passions for the strong:
So, when small humours gather to a gout,
The doctor fancies he has driven them out.
    Yes, Nature's road must ever be preferr'd;
Reason is here no guide, but still a guard;
'Tis hers to rectify, not overthrow,
And treat this passion more as friend than foe:
A mightier power the strong direction sends,
And several men impels to several ends:
Like varying winds, by other passions toss'd,
This drives them constant to a certain coast.
Let power or knowledge, gold or glory please,
Or (oft more strong than all) the love of ease;
Through life 'tis follow'd, even at life's expense;
The merchant's toil, the sage's indolence,
The monk's humility, the hero's pride,
All, all alike find reason on their side.
    The eternal art educing good from ill,
Grafts on this passion our best principle:
'Tis thus the mercury of man is fix'd,
Strong grows the virtue with his nature mix'd;
The dross cements what else were too refined,
And in one interest body acts with mind.
    As fruits, ungrateful to the planter's care,

On savage stocks inserted learn to bear;
The surest virtues thus from passions shoot,
Wild Nature's vigour working at the root.
What crops of wit and honesty appear
From spleen, from obstinacy, hate, or fear!
See anger, zeal and fortitude supply;
Even av'rice, prudence; sloth, philosophy;
Lust, through some certain strainers well refined,
Is gentle love, and charms all womankind;
Envy, to which the ignoble mind's a slave,
Is emulation in the learn'd or brave;
Nor virtue, male or female, can we name,
But what will grow on pride, or grow on shame.
    Thus Nature gives us (let it check our pride)
The virtue nearest to our vice allied:
Reason the bias turns to good from ill,
And Nero reigns a Titus, if he will.
The fiery soul abhorr'd in Catiline,
In Decius charms, in Curtius is divine:
The same ambition can destroy or save,
And makes a patriot as it makes a knave.
    IV. This light and darkness in our chaos join'd,
What shall divide? The God within the mind.
    Extremes in Nature equal ends produce,
In man they join to some mysterious use;
Though each by turns the other's bounds invade,
As, in some well-wrought picture, light and shade,
And oft so mix, the difference is too nice
Where ends the virtue or begins the vice.
    Fools! who from hence into the notion fall
That vice or virtue there is none at all.
If white and black blend, soften, and unite
A thousand ways, is there no black or white?
Ask your own heart, and nothing is so plain;
'Tis to mistake them, costs the time and pain.
    V. Vice is a monster of so frightful mien,
As, to be hated, needs but to be seen;
Yet seen too oft, familiar with her face,
We first endure, then pity, then embrace.
But where the extreme of vice, was ne'er agreed:
Ask where's the north? at York, 'tis on the Tweed;

In Scotland, at the Orcades; and there,
At Greenland, Zembla, or the Lord knows where.
No creature owns it in the first degree,
But thinks his neighbour farther gone than he:
Even those who dwell beneath its very zone,
Or never feel the rage, or never own;
What happier natures shrink at with affright,
The hard inhabitant contends is right.

    VI. Virtuous and vicious every man must be,
Few in the extreme, but all in the degree;
The rogue and fool by fits is fair and wise;
And even the best by fits what they despise.
'Tis but by parts we follow good or ill;
For, vice or virtue, self directs it still;
Each individual seeks a several goal;
But Heaven's great view is one, and that the whole,
That counter-works each folly and caprice
That disappoints the effect of every vice;
That, happy frailties to all ranks applied:
Shame to the virgin, to the matron pride,
Fear to the statesman, rashness to the chief;
To kings presumption, and to crowds belief:
That, virtue's ends from vanity can raise,
Which seeks no interest, no reward but praise;
And build on wants, and on defects of mind,
The joy, the peace, the glory of mankind.

    Heaven forming each on other to depend,
A master, or a servant, or a friend,
Bids each on other for assistance call,
Till one man's weakness grows the strength of all.
Wants, frailties, passions, closer still ally
The common interest, or endear the tie.
To these we owe true friendship, love sincere,
Each homefelt joy that life inherits here;
Yet from the same we learn, in its decline,
Those joys, those loves, those interests to resign;
Taught half by reason, half by mere decay,
To welcome death, and calmly pass away.

    Whate'er the passion, knowledge, fame, or pelf,
Not one will change his neighbour with himself.
The learn'd is happy Nature to explore,

The fool is happy that he knows no more;
The rich is happy in the plenty given,
The poor contents him with the care of Heaven.
See the blind beggar dance, the cripple sing,
The sot a hero, lunatic a king;
The starving chemist in his golden views
Supremely blest, the poet in his muse.
See some strange comfort every state attend,
And pride bestow'd on all, a common friend:
See some fit passion every age supply,
Hope travels through, nor quits us when we die.
　Behold the child, by Nature's kindly law,
Pleased with a rattle, tickled with a straw:
Some livelier plaything gives his youth delight,
A little louder, but as empty quite:
Scarfs, garters, gold, amuse his riper stage,
And beads and prayer-books are the toys of age:
Pleased with this bauble still, as that before;
Till tired he sleeps, and life's poor play is o'er.
Meanwhile opinion gilds with varying rays
Those painted clouds that beautify our days;
Each want of happiness by hope supplied,
And each vacuity of sense by pride:
These build as fast as knowledge can destroy;
In folly's cup still laughs the bubble, joy;
One prospect lost, another still we gain;
And not a vanity is given in vain;
Even mean self-love becomes, by force divine,
The scale to measure others' wants by thine.
See! and confess, one comfort still must rise;
'Tis this, — though man's a fool, yet God is wise.

EPISTLE III

Argument

OF THE NATURE AND STATE OF MAN WITH RESPECT TO SOCIETY

　I. The whole universe one system of society, ver. 7, etc. Nothing made wholly for itself, nor yet wholly for another, ver. 27. The happiness of animals mutual, ver. 49. II. Reason or instinct operate alike to the good of each individual, ver. 79. Reason or instinct operate also to society in all animals, ver. 109. III. How far society carried by instinct, ver. 115. How much farther by reason, ver. 128. IV. Of that which is called the state of nature, ver. 144. Reason instructed by instinct in the invention of arts, ver. 166, and in the forms of society, ver. 176. V. Origin of political societies, ver. 196. Origin of monarchy, ver. 207. Patriarchal government, ver. 212. VI. Origin of true religion and government, from the same principle of love, ver. 231, etc. Origin of superstition and tyranny, from the same principle of fear, ver. 237, etc. The influence of self-love operating to the social and public good, ver. 266. Restoration of true religion and government on their first principle, ver. 285. Mixed government, ver. 288. Various forms of each, and the true end of all, ver. 300, etc.

Here then we rest: "The Universal Cause
Acts to one end, but acts by various laws."
In all the madness of superfluous health,
The trim of pride, the impudence of wealth,
Let this great truth be present night and day;
But most be present if we preach or pray.
   Look round our world; behold the chain of love
Combining all below and all above.
See plastic Nature working to this end,
The single atoms each to other tend,
Attract, attracted to, the next in place
Form'd and impell'd its neighbour to embrace.
See Matter next, with various life endued,
Press to one centre still, the general good.
See dying vegetables life sustain,
See life dissolving vegetate again:
All forms that perish other forms supply;
(By turns we catch the vital breath, and die)
Like bubbles on the sea of Matter borne,
They rise, they break, and to that sea return.
Nothing is foreign: parts relate to whole;
One all-extending, all-preserving soul
Connects each being, greatest with the least;
Made beast in aid of man, and man of beast;
All served, all serving: nothing stands alone:
The chain holds on, and where it ends, unknown.
   Has God, thou fool! work'd solely for thy good,
Thy joy, thy pastime, thy attire, thy food?
Who for thy table feeds the wanton fawn,
For him as kindly spread the flowery lawn:
Is it for thee the lark ascends and sings?

Joy tunes his voice, joy elevates his wings.   — *not really*
Is it for thee the linnet pours his throat?
Loves of his own and raptures swell the note.
The bounding steed you pompously bestride
Shares with his lord the pleasure and the pride.
Is thine alone the seed that strews the plain?
The birds of heaven shall vindicate their grain.
Thine the full harvest of the golden year?
Part pays, and justly, the deserving steer:
The hog, that ploughs not, nor obeys thy call,
Lives on the labours of this lord of all.
    Know, Nature's children all divide her care;
The fur that warms a monarch warm'd a bear.
While man exclaims, "See all things for my use!"
"See man for mine!" replies a pamper'd goose:
And just as short of reason he must fall,
Who thinks all made for one, not one for all.
    Grant that the powerful still the weak control;
Be man the wit and tyrant of the whole:
Nature that tyrant checks; he only knows,
And helps, another creature's wants and woes.
Say, will the falcon, stooping from above,
Smit with her varying plumage, spare the dove?
Admires the jay the insect's gilded wings?
Or hears the hawk when Philomela sings?
Man cares for all: to birds he gives his woods,
To beasts his pastures, and to fish his floods;
For some his interest prompts him to provide,
For more his pleasure, yet for more his pride:
All feed on one vain patron, and enjoy
The extensive blessing of his luxury.
That very life his learned hunger craves,
He saves from famine, from the savage saves:
Nay, feasts the animal he dooms his feast,
And, till he ends the being, makes it bless'd;
Which sees no more the stroke, or feels the pain,
Than favour'd man by touch ethereal slain.
The creature had his feast of life before;
Thou too must perish when thy feast is o'er!
    To each unthinking being, Heaven, a friend,
Gives not the useless knowledge of its end:

To man imparts it; but with such a view
As, while he dreads it, makes him hope it too:
The hour conceal'd, and so remote the fear,
Death still draws nearer, never seeming near.
Great standing miracle! that Heaven assign'd
Its only thinking thing this turn of mind.

II. Whether with reason or with instinct blest,
Know, all enjoy that power which suits them best;
To bliss alike by that direction tend,
And find the means proportion'd to their end.
Say, where full instinct is the unerring guide,
What pope or council can they need beside?
Reason, however able, cool at best,
Cares not for service, or but serves when press'd,
Stays till we call, and then not often near;
But honest instinct comes a volunteer,
Sure never to o'ershoot, but just to hit;
While still too wide or short is human wit;
Sure by quick nature happiness to gain,
Which heavier reason labours at in vain.
This too serves always, reason never long;
One must go right, the other may go wrong.
See then the acting and comparing powers
One in their nature, which are two in ours;
And reason raise o'er instinct as you can,
In this 'tis God directs, in that 'tis man.

Who taught the nations of the field and wood
To shun their poison, and to choose their food?
Prescient, the tides or tempests to withstand,
Build on the wave, or arch beneath the sand?
Who made the spider parallels design,
Sure as De Moivre, without rule or line?
Who bade the stork, Columbus-like, explore
Heavens not his own, and worlds unknown before?
Who calls the council, states the certain day,
Who forms the phalanx, and who points the way?

III. God, in the nature of each being, founds
Its proper bliss, and sets its proper bounds:
But as He framed a whole, the whole to bless,
On mutual wants built mutual happiness:
So from the first eternal Order ran,

And creature link'd to creature, man to man.
Whate'er of life all-quick'ning ether keeps,
Or breathes through air, or shoots beneath the deeps,
Or pours profuse on earth, one nature feeds
The vital flame, and swells the genial seeds.
Not man alone, but all that roam the wood,
Or wing the sky, or roll along the flood,
Each loves itself, but not itself alone,
Each sex desires alike, till two are one.
Nor ends the pleasure with the fierce embrace:
They love themselves, a third time, in their race.
Thus beast and bird their common charge attend,
The mothers nurse it, and the sires defend;
The young dismiss'd to wander earth or air,
There stops the instinct, and there ends the care;
The link dissolves, each seeks a fresh embrace,
Another love succeeds, another race.
A longer care man's helpless kind demands;
That longer care contracts more lasting bands:
Reflection, reason, still the ties improve,
At once extend the interest, and the love:
With choice we fix, with sympathy we burn;
Each virtue in each passion takes its turn;
And still new needs, new helps, new habits rise,
That graft benevolence on charities.
Still as one brood, and as another rose,
These natural love maintain'd, habitual those:
The last, scarce ripen'd into perfect man,
Saw helpless him from whom their life began:
Memory and forecast just returns engage,
That pointed back to youth, this on to age;
While pleasure, gratitude, and hope combined,
Still spread the interest and preserved the kind.
    IV. Nor think, in Nature's state they blindly trod;
The state of Nature was the reign of God:
Self-love and social at her birth began,
Union the bond of all things, and of man.
Pride then was not; nor arts, that pride to aid;
Man walk'd with beast, joint tenant of the shade;
The same his table, and the same his bed;
No murder clothed him, and no murder fed.

In the same temple, the resounding wood,
All vocal beings hymn'd their equal God:
The shrine with gore unstain'd, with gold undress'd,
Unbribed, unbloody, stood the blameless priest:
Heaven's attribute was universal care,
And man's prerogative, to rule, but spare.
Ah! how unlike the man of times to come!
Of half that live the butcher and the tomb;
Who, foe to Nature, hears the general groan,
Murders their species, and betrays his own.
But just disease to luxury succeeds,
And every death its own avenger breeds;
The fury-passions from that blood began,
And turn'd on man, a fiercer savage, man.
    See him from Nature rising slow to Art!
To copy instinct then was reason's part;
Thus then to man the voice of Nature spake:
"Go, from the creatures thy instructions take:
Learn from the birds what food the thickets yield;
Learn from the beasts the physic of the field;
Thy arts of building from the bee receive;
Learn of the mole to plough, the worm to weave;
Learn of the little nautilus to sail,
Spread the thin oar, and catch the driving gale.
Here too all forms of social union find,
And hence let reason, late, instruct mankind:
Here subterranean works and cities see;
There towns aerial on the waving tree.
Learn each small people's genius, policies,
The ants' republic, and the realm of bees;
How those in common all their wealth bestow,
And anarchy without confusion know;
And these for ever, though a monarch reign,
Their separate cells and properties maintain.
Mark what unvaried laws preserve each state,
Laws wise as Nature, and as fix'd as fate.
In vain thy reason finer webs shall draw,
Entangle Justice in her net of law,
And right, too rigid, harden into wrong;
Still for the strong too weak, the weak too strong.
Yet go! and thus o'er all the creatures sway,

Thus let the wiser make the rest obey:
And for those arts mere instinct could afford,
Be crown'd as monarchs, or as gods adored."
    V. Great Nature spoke; observant men obey'd;
Cities were built, societies were made:
Here rose one little state; another near
Grew by like means, and join'd, through love or fear.
Did here the trees with ruddier burdens bend,
And there the streams in purer rills descend?
What war could ravish, commerce could bestow,
And he return'd a friend, who came a foe.
Converse and love mankind might strongly draw,
When love was liberty, and nature law.
Thus states were form'd; the name of king unknown,
Till common interest placed the sway in one.
'Twas virtue only (or in arts or arms,
Diffusing blessings, or averting harms),
The same which in a sire the sons obey'd,
A prince the father of a people made.
    VI. Till then, by Nature crown'd, each patriarch sate,
King, priest, and parent of his growing state;
On him, their second Providence, they hung,
Their law his eye, their oracle his tongue.
He from the wondering furrow call'd the food,
Taught to command the fire, control the flood,
Draw forth the monsters of the abyss profound,
Or fetch the aerial eagle to the ground.
Till drooping, sickening, dying, they began
Whom they revered as God to mourn as man:
Then, looking up from sire to sire, explored
One great first Father, and that first adored.
Or plain tradition that this all begun,
Convey'd unbroken faith from sire to son;
The worker from the work distinct was known,
And simple reason never sought but one:
Ere wit oblique had broke that steady light,
Man, like his Maker, saw that all was right;
To virtue, in the paths of pleasure trod,
And own'd a Father when he own'd a God.
Love, all the faith and all the allegiance then;
For Nature knew no right divine in men,

No ill could fear in God; and understood
A sovereign Being, but a sovereign good:
True faith, true policy, united ran,
That was but love of God, and this of man.
  Who first taught souls enslaved, and realms undone,
The enormous faith of many made for one;
That proud exception to all Nature's laws,
To invert the world, and counter-work its cause?
Force first made conquest, and that conquest, law;
Till Superstition taught the tyrant awe,
Then shared the tyranny, then lent it aid,
And gods of conquerors, slaves of subjects made:
She midst the lightning's blaze, and thunder's sound,
When rock'd the mountains, and when groan'd the ground,
She taught the weak to bend, the proud to pray,
To power unseen, and mightier far than they:
She, from the rending earth and bursting skies,
Saw gods descend, and fiends infernal rise:
Here fix'd the dreadful, there the blest abodes:
Fear made her devils, and weak hope her gods;
Gods partial, changeful, passionate, unjust,
Whose attributes were rage, revenge, or lust;
Such as the souls of cowards might conceive,
And, form'd like tyrants, tyrants would believe.
Zeal then, not charity, became the guide;
And hell was built on spite, and heaven on pride.
Then sacred seem'd the ethereal vault no more;
Altars grew marble then, and reek'd with gore:
Then first the flamen tasted living food;
Next his grim idol smear'd with human blood;
With Heaven's own thunders shook the world below,
And play'd the god an engine on his foe.
  So drives self-love through just and through unjust,
To one man's power, ambition, lucre, lust:
The same self-love, in all, becomes the cause
Of what restrains him, government and laws.
For, what one likes, if others like as well,
What serves one will, when many wills rebel?
How shall he keep, what, sleeping or awake,
A weaker may surprise, a stronger take?
His safety must his liberty restrain:

All join to guard what each desires to gain.
Forced into virtue thus, by self-defence,
Even kings learn'd justice and benevolence:
Self-love forsook the path it first pursued,
And found the private in the public good.
    'Twas then the studious head or generous mind,
Follower of God, or friend of human kind,
Poet or patriot, rose but to restore
The faith and moral Nature gave before;
Relumed her ancient light, not kindled new,
If not God's image, yet his shadow drew;
Taught power's due use to people and to kings,
Taught nor to slack, nor strain its tender strings,
The less, or greater, set so justly true,
That touching one must strike the other too:
Till jarring interests of themselves create
The according music of a well-mix'd state.
Such is the world's great harmony, that springs
From order, union, full consent of things:
Where small and great, where weak and mighty, made
To serve, not suffer — strengthen, not invade;
More powerful each as needful to the rest,
And, in proportion as it blesses, blest;
Draw to one point, and to one centre bring
Beast, man, or angel, servant, lord, or king.
    For forms of government let fools contest:
Whate'er is best administer'd is best:
For modes of faith, let graceless zealots fight;
His can't be wrong whose life is in the right;
In faith and hope the world will disagree,
But all mankind's concern is charity:
All must be false that thwart this one great end:
And all of God that bless mankind or mend.
Man, like the generous vine, supported lives:
The strength he gains is from the embrace he gives.
On their own axis as the planets run,
Yet make at once their circle round the sun;
So two consistent motions act the soul;
And one regards itself, and one the whole.
    Thus God and Nature link'd the general frame,
And bade self-love and social be the same.

EPISTLE IV

Argument

OF THE NATURE AND STATE OF MAN WITH RESPECT TO HAPPINESS

   I. False notions of happiness, philosophical and popular, answered from ver. 19 to 27. II. It is the end of all men, and attainable by all, ver. 29. God intends happiness to be equal; and to be so it must be social, since all particular happiness depends on general, and since He governs by general, not particular, laws, ver. 35. As it is necessary for order, and the peace and welfare of society, that external goods should be unequal, happiness is not made to consist in these, ver. 51. But notwithstanding that inequality, the balance of happiness among mankind is kept even by Providence by the two passions of hope and fear, ver. 70. III. What the happiness of individuals is, as far as is consistent with the constitution of this world; and that the good man has here the advantage, ver. 77. The error of imputing to virtue what are only the calamities of Nature or of Fortune, ver. 94. IV. The folly of expecting that God should alter His general laws in favour of particulars, ver. 121. V. That we are not judges who are good; but that, whoever they are, they must be happiest, ver. 131, etc. VI. That external goods are not the proper rewards, but often inconsistent with, or destructive of virtue, ver. 167. That even these can make no man happy without virtue: instanced in riches, ver. 185. Honours, ver. 193. Nobility, ver. 205. Greatness, ver. 217. Fame, ver. 237. Superior talents, ver. 259, etc. With pictures of human infelicity in men possessed of them all, ver. 269, etc. VII. That virtue only constitutes a happiness whose object is universal, and whose prospect eternal, ver. 309. That the perfection of virtue and happiness consists in a conformity to the order of Providence here, and a resignation to it here and hereafter, ver. 326, etc.

> Oh Happiness! our being's end and aim!
> Good, pleasure, ease, content! whate'er thy name:
> That something still which prompts the eternal sigh,
> For which we bear to live, or dare to die,
> Which still so near us, yet beyond us lies,
> O'erlook'd, seen double, by the fool and wise.
> Plant of celestial seed! if dropp'd below,
> Say, in what mortal soil thou deign'st to grow?
> Fair opening to some court's propitious shine,
> Or deep with diamonds in the flaming mine?
> Twined with the wreaths Parnassian laurels yield,
> Or reap'd in iron harvests of the field?
> Where grows? where grows it not? If vain our toil,
> We ought to blame the culture, not the soil:

Fix'd to no spot is happiness sincere,
'Tis nowhere to be found, or everywhere:
'Tis never to be bought, but always free,
And, fled from monarchs, St. John! dwells with thee.
    Ask of the learn'd the way? the learn'd are blind;
This bids to serve, and that to shun, mankind;
Some place the bliss in action, some in ease,
Those call it pleasure, and contentment these;
Some, sunk to beasts, find pleasure end in pain;
Some, swell'd to gods, confess even virtue vain;
Or, indolent, to each extreme they fall,
To trust in everything, or doubt of all.
    Who thus define it, say they more or less
Than this, that happiness is happiness?
    II. Take Nature's path, and mad opinions leave;
All states can reach it, and all heads conceive;
Obvious her goods, in no extreme they dwell;
There needs but thinking right, and meaning well;
And, mourn our various portions as we please,
Equal is common sense and common ease.
    Remember, man, "The Universal Cause
Acts not by partial, but by general laws";
And makes what happiness we justly call
Subsist, not in the good of one, but all.
There's not a blessing individuals find,
But some way leans and hearkens to the kind:
No bandit fierce, no tyrant mad with pride,
No cavern'd hermit, rests self-satisfied:
Who most to shun or hate mankind pretend,
Seek an admirer, or would fix a friend:
Abstract what others feel, what others think,
All pleasures sicken, and all glories sink;
Each has his share; and who would more obtain,
Shall find the pleasure pays not half the pain.
    Order is Heaven's first law; and, this confess'd,
Some are, and must be, greater than the rest,
More rich, more wise; but who infers from hence
That such are happier, shocks all common sense.
Heaven to mankind impartial we confess,
If all are equal in their happiness:
But mutual wants this happiness increase;

All nature's difference keeps all nature's peace.
Condition, circumstance, is not the thing;
Bliss is the same in subject or in king,
In who obtain defence, or who defend,
In him who is, or him who finds a friend:
Heaven breathes through every member of the whole
One common blessing, as one common soul.
But fortune's gifts, if each alike possess'd,
And each were equal, must not all contest?
If then to all men happiness was meant,
God in externals could not place content.

    Fortune her gifts may variously dispose,
And these be happy call'd, unhappy those;
But Heaven's just balance equal will appear,
While those are placed in hope, and these in fear:
Not present good or ill, the joy or curse,
But future views of better or of worse.

    Oh sons of earth! attempt ye still to rise,
By mountains piled on mountains, to the skies?
Heaven still with laughter the vain toil surveys,
And buries madmen in the heaps they raise.

    III. Know, all the good that individuals find,
Or God and Nature meant to mere mankind,
Reason's whole pleasure, all the joys of sense,
Lie in three words — health, peace, and competence.
But health consists with temperance alone;
And peace, O Virtue! peace is all thy own.
The good or bad the gifts of fortune gain;
But these less taste them as they worse obtain.
Say, in pursuit of profit or delight,
Who risk the most, that take wrong means, or right?
Of vice or virtue, whether blest or curst,
Which meets contempt, or which compassion first?
Count all the advantage prosperous vice attains,
'Tis but what virtue flies from and disdains:
And grant the bad what happiness they would,
One they must want, which is, to pass for good.
Oh blind to truth, and God's whole scheme below,
Who fancy bliss to vice, to virtue woe!
Who sees and follows that great scheme the best,
Best knows the blessing, and will most be blest.

But fools, the good alone unhappy call,
For ills or accidents that chance to all.
See Falkland dies, the virtuous and the just!
See godlike Turenne prostrate on the dust!
See Sidney bleeds amid the martial strife!
Was this their virtue, or contempt of life?
Say, was it virtue, more though Heaven ne'er gave,
Lamented Digby! sunk thee to the grave?
Tell me, if virtue made the son expire,
Why, full of days and honour, lives the sire?
Why drew Marseilles' good bishop[15] purer breath,
When nature sicken'd, and each gale was death?
Or why so long (in life if long can be)
Lent Heaven a parent to the poor and me?
    What makes all physical or moral ill?
There deviates nature, and here wanders will.
God sends not ill; if rightly understood,
Or partial ill is universal good,
Or change admits, or nature lets it fall,
Short, and but rare, 'till man improved it all.
We just as wisely might of Heaven complain
That righteous Abel was destroy'd by Cain,
As that the virtuous son is ill at ease
When his lewd father gave the dire disease.
    IV. Think we, like some weak prince, the Eternal Cause
Prone for His favourites to reverse His laws?
Shall burning Ætna, if a sage requires,
Forget to thunder, and recall her fires?
On air or sea new motions be impress'd,
Oh blameless Bethel! to relieve thy breast?[16]
When the loose mountain trembles from on high,
Shall gravitation cease if you go by?
Or some old temple, nodding to its fall,
For Chartres' head reserve the hanging wall?
    V. But still this world (so fitted for the knave)
Contents us not. A better shall we have?
A kingdom of the just then let it be:

---

[15] M. de Belsunce, a public benefactor during the plague of 1720.
[16] Hugh Bethel, a friend of Pope and victim of asthma.

But first consider how those just agree.
The good must merit God's peculiar care!
But who but God can tell us who they are?
One thinks on Calvin Heaven's own spirit fell,
Another deems him instrument of hell;
If Calvin feel Heaven's blessing, or its rod,
This cries, There is, and that, There is no God.
What shocks one part will edify the rest,
Nor with one system can they all be blest.
The very best will variously incline,
And what rewards your virtue, punish mine.
Whatever is, is right. — This world, 'tis true,
Was made for Cæsar — but for Titus too;
And which more blest? who chain'd his country, say,
Or he whose virtue sigh'd to lose a day?
    "But sometimes virtue starves, while vice is fed."
What then? is the reward of virtue bread?
That, vice may merit, 'tis the price of toil;
The knave deserves it, when he tills the soil,
The knave deserves it, when he tempts the main,
Where folly fights for kings, or dives for gain.
The good man may be weak, be indolent;
Nor is his claim to plenty, but content.
But grant him riches, your demand is o'er?
"No — shall the good want health, the good want power?"
Add health and power, and every earthly thing,
"Why bounded power? why private? why no king?"
Nay, why external for internal given?
Why is not man a god, and earth a heaven?
Who ask and reason thus will scarce conceive
God gives enough while He has more to give;
Immense the power, immense were the demand;
Say, at what part of nature will they stand?
    VI. What nothing earthly gives, or can destroy,
The soul's calm sunshine, and the heartfelt joy,
Is virtue's prize: a better would you fix?
Then give humility a coach and six,
Justice a conqueror's sword, or truth a gown,
Or public spirit its great cure, a crown.
Weak, foolish man! will Heaven reward us there
With the same trash mad mortals wish for here?

The boy and man an individual makes,
Yet sigh'st thou now for apples and for cakes?
Go, like the Indian, in another life
Expect thy dog, thy bottle, and thy wife;
As well as dream such trifles are assign'd,
As toys and empires, for a godlike mind.
Rewards, that either would to virtue bring
No joy, or be destructive of the thing:
How oft by these at sixty are undone
The virtues of a saint at twenty-one!
To whom can riches give repute, or trust,
Content, or pleasure, but the good and just?
Judges and senates have been bought for gold,
Esteem and love were never to be sold.
O fool! to think God hates the worthy mind,
The lover and the love of human kind,
Whose life is healthful, and whose conscience clear,
Because he wants a thousand pounds a year.
　　Honour and shame from no condition rise:
Act well your part; there all the honour lies.
Fortune in men has some small difference made,
One flaunts in rags, one flutters in brocade;
The cobbler apron'd, and the parson gown'd,
The friar hooded, and the monarch crown'd.
"What differ more (you cry) than crown and cowl?"
I'll tell you, friend! a wise man and a fool.
You'll find, if once the monarch acts the monk,
Or, cobbler-like, the parson will be drunk,
Worth makes the man, and want of it the fellow:
The rest is all but leather or prunella.
　　Stuck o'er with titles and hung round with strings,
That thou may'st be by kings or whores of kings,
Boast the pure blood of an illustrious race,
In quiet flow from Lucrece to Lucrece:
But by your father's worth if yours you rate,
Count me those only who were good and great.
Go! if your ancient but ignoble blood
Has crept through scoundrels ever since the flood,
Go! and pretend your family is young;
Nor own your fathers have been fools so long.
What can ennoble sots, or slaves, or cowards?

Alas! not all the blood of all the Howards.
    Look next on greatness; say where greatness lies.
Where, but among the heroes and the wise?
Heroes are much the same, the point's agreed,
From Macedonia's madman to the Swede;[17]
The whole strange purpose of their lives to find
Or make an enemy of all mankind!
Not one looks backward, onward still he goes,
Yet ne'er looks forward farther than his nose.
No less alike the politic and wise;
All sly slow things, with circumspective eyes:
Men in their loose unguarded hours they take,
Not that themselves are wise, but others weak.
But grant that those can conquer, these can cheat;
'Tis phrase absurd to call a villain great:
Who wickedly is wise, or madly brave,
Is but the more a fool, the more a knave.
Who noble ends by noble means obtains,
Or failing, smiles in exile or in chains,
Like good Aurelius let him reign, or bleed
Like Socrates, that man is great indeed.
    What's fame? A fancied life in others' breath,
A thing beyond us, even before our death.
Just what you hear, you have, and what's unknown
The same (my lord) if Tully's,[18] or your own.
All that we feel of it begins and ends
In the small circle of our foes or friends;
To all beside as much an empty shade
An Eugene[19] living, as a Cæsar dead;
Alike or when, or where, they shone, or shine,
Or on the Rubicon, or on the Rhine.
A wit's a feather, and a chief's a rod;
An honest man's the noblest work of God.
Fame but from death a villain's name can save,
As Justice tears his body from the grave!
When what to oblivion better were resign'd

[17] Alexander the Great and Charles XII of Sweden.
[18] Cicero.
[19] The Austrian general Eugene of Savoy.

Is hung on high to poison half mankind.
All fame is foreign, but of true desert;
Plays round the head, but comes not to the heart:
One self-approving hour whole years outweighs
Of stupid starers, and of loud huzzas;
And more true joy Marcellus exiled feels,
Than Cæsar with a senate at his heels.
    In parts superior what advantage lies?
Tell (for you can) what is it to be wise?
'Tis but to know how little can be known;
To see all others' faults and feel our own:
Condemn'd in business or in arts to drudge,
Without a second or without a judge:
Truths would you teach, or save a sinking land?
All fear, none aid you, and few understand.
Painful pre-eminence! yourself to view
Above life's weakness, and its comforts too.
    Bring then these blessings to a strict account;
Make fair deductions; see to what they mount:
How much of other each is sure to cost;
How each for other oft is wholly lost;
How inconsistent greater goods with these;
How sometimes life is risk'd, and always ease:
Think, and if still the things thy envy call,
Say, wouldst thou be the man to whom they fall?
To sigh for ribands if thou art so silly,
Mark how they grace Lord Umbra or Sir Billy.
Is yellow dirt the passion of thy life?
Look but on Gripus or on Gripus' wife.
If parts allure thee, think how Bacon shined,
The wisest, brightest, meanest of mankind:
Or, ravish'd with the whistling of a name,
See Cromwell, damn'd to everlasting fame!
If all, united, thy ambition call,
From ancient story, learn to scorn them all.
There, in the rich, the honour'd, famed, and great,
See the false scale of happiness complete!
In hearts of kings, or arms of queens, who lay,
How happy those to ruin, these betray.
Mark by what wretched steps their glory grows,
From dirt and sea-weed as proud Venice rose;

In each how guilt and greatness equal ran,
And all that raised the hero sunk the man:
Now Europe's laurels on their brows behold,
But stain'd with blood, or ill exchanged for gold:
Then see them broke with toils, or sunk in ease,
Or infamous for plunder'd provinces.
Oh wealth ill-fated! which no act of fame
E'er taught to shine, or sanctified from shame!
What greater bliss attends their close of life?
Some greedy minion, or imperious wife,
The trophied arches, storied halls invade,
And haunt their slumbers in the pompous shade.
Alas! not dazzled with their noontide ray,
Compute the morn and evening to the day:
The whole amount of that enormous fame,
A tale that blends their glory with their shame!
  VII. Know then this truth (enough for man to know),
"Virtue alone is happiness below."
The only point where human bliss stands still,
And tastes the good without the fall to ill;
Where only merit constant pay receives,
Is blest in what it takes and what it gives;
The joy unequall'd, if its end it gain,
And if it lose, attended with no pain:
Without satiety, though e'er so bless'd,
And but more relish'd as the more distress'd:
The broadest mirth unfeeling folly wears,
Less pleasing far than virtue's very tears:
Good, from each object, from each place acquired,
For ever exercised, yet never tired;
Never elated while one man's oppress'd;
Never dejected while another's bless'd;
And where no wants, no wishes can remain,
Since but to wish more virtue, is to gain.
  See the sole bliss Heaven could on all bestow;
Which who but feels can taste, but thinks can know.
Yet poor with fortune, and with learning blind,
The bad must miss, the good, untaught, will find;
Slave to no sect, who takes no private road,
But looks through Nature up to Nature's God:
Pursues that chain which links the immense design,

Joins Heaven and earth, and mortal and divine;
Sees that no being any bliss can know,
But touches some above, and some below;
Learns, from this union of the rising whole,
The first, last purpose of the human soul;
And knows where faith, law, morals, all began,
All end, in love of God, and love of man.
For him alone, hope leads from goal to goal,
And opens still, and opens on his soul;
Till lengthen'd on to faith, and unconfined,
It pours the bliss that fills up all the mind.
He sees why nature plants in man alone
Hope of known bliss, and faith in bliss unknown:
(Nature, whose dictates to no other kind
Are given in vain, but what they seek they find;)
Wise is her present; she connects in this
His greatest virtue with his greatest bliss;
At once his own bright prospect to be blest,
And strongest motive to assist the rest.
    Self-love thus push'd to social, to divine,
Gives thee to make thy neighbour's blessing thine.
Is this too little for the boundless heart?
Extend it, let thy enemies have part:
Grasp the whole worlds of reason, life, and sense,
In one close system of benevolence:
Happier as kinder, in whate'er degree,
And height of bliss but height of charity.
    God loves from whole to parts: but human soul
Must rise from individual to the whole.
Self-love but serves the virtuous mind to wake,
As the small pebble stirs the peaceful lake;
The centre moved, a circle straight succeeds,
Another still, and still another spreads;
Friend, parent, neighbour, first it will embrace;
His country next; and next all human race;
Wide and more wide, the o'erflowings of the mind
Take every creature in, of every kind;
Earth smiles around, with boundless bounty blest,
And Heaven beholds its image in his breast.
    Come, then, my friend! my genius! come along;
Oh master of the poet and the song!

· And while the Muse now stoops, or now ascends,
To man's low passions, or their glorious ends,
Teach me, like thee, in various nature wise,
To fall with dignity, with temper rise;
Form'd by thy converse happily to steer
From grave to gay, from lively to severe;
Correct, with spirit; eloquent, with ease;
Intent to reason, or polite to please.
Oh! while along the stream of time thy name
Expanded flies, and gathers all its fame;
Say, shall my little bark attendant sail,
Pursue the triumph, and partake the gale?
When statesmen, heroes, kings, in dust repose,
Whose sons shall blush their fathers were thy foes,
Shall then this verse to future age pretend
Thou wert my guide, philosopher, and friend?
That, urged by thee, I turn'd the tuneful art
From sounds to things, from fancy to the heart;
For Wit's false mirror held up Nature's light;
Show'd erring Pride, — Whatever is, is right!
That reason, passion, answer one great aim;
That true self-love and social are the same;
That virtue only makes our bliss below;
And all our knowledge is, — Ourselves to know.

V

EPISTLE IV

To Richard Boyle, Earl of Burlington

Argument

OF THE USE OF RICHES

The vanity of expense in people of wealth and quality. The abuse of the word taste, ver. 13. That the first principle and foundation in this, as in everything else, is good sense, ver. 39. The chief proof of it is to follow Nature, even in works of mere luxury and elegance. Instanced in architecture and gardening, where all must be adapted to the genius and use of the place, and the beauties not forced into it, but resulting from it, ver. 47. How men are disappointed in their most expensive undertakings for want of this true foundation, without which nothing can please long, if at all; and the best examples and rules will be but perverted into something burdensome or ridiculous, ver. 65, etc., to 98. A description of the false taste of magnificence; the first grand error of which is to imagine that greatness consists in the size and dimensions, instead of the proportion and harmony of the whole, ver. 99; and the second, either in joining together parts incoherent, or too minutely resembling, or in the repetition of the same too frequently, ver. 105, etc. A word or two of false taste in books, in music, in painting, even in preaching and prayer, and lastly in entertainments, ver. 133, etc. Yet Providence is justified in giving wealth to be squandered in this manner, since it is dispersed to the poor and laborious part of mankind, ver. 169 (recurring to what is laid down in the *Essay on Man*, Epistle II., and in the epistle preceding, ver. 159, etc.). What are the proper objects of magnificence, and a proper field for the expense of great men, ver. 177, etc.; and finally, the great and public works which become a prince, ver. 191 to the end.

'Tis strange, the miser should his cares employ
To gain those riches he can ne'er enjoy:
Is it less strange, the prodigal should waste
His wealth to purchase what he ne'er can taste?
Not for himself he sees, or hears, or eats;
Artists must choose his pictures, music, meats:
He buys for Topham[20] drawings and designs,
For Pembroke statues, dirty gods, and coins;
Rare monkish manuscripts for Hearne alone,
And books for Mead, and butterflies for Sloane.
Think we all these are for himself? no more
Than his fine wife, alas! or finer whore.
    For what has Virro painted, built, and planted?
Only to show how many tastes he wanted.
What brought Sir Visto's ill-got wealth to waste?
Some demon whisper'd, "Visto! have a taste."
Heaven visits with a taste the wealthy fool,
And needs no rod but Ripley[21] with a rule.
See! sportive Fate, to punish awkward pride,
Bids Bubo[22] build, and sends him such a guide:
A standing sermon, at each year's expense,
That never coxcomb reach'd magnificence!

---

[20] Topham; the Earl of Pembroke; Hearne; Mead; Sir Hans Sloane: famous contemporary collectors.
[21] The architect Thomas Ripley.
[22] Bubb Dodington, Lord Melcombe.

You show us Rome was glorious, not profuse,
And pompous buildings once were things of use.
Yet shall (my lord) your just, your noble rules
Fill half the land with imitating fools;
Who random drawings from your sheets shall take,
And of one beauty many blunders make;
Load some vain church with old theatric state,
Turn acts of triumph to a garden-gate;
Reverse your ornaments, and hang them all
On some patch'd dog-hole eked with ends of wall;
Then clap four slices of pilaster on 't,
That, laced with bits of rustic, makes a front.
Shall call the winds through long arcades to roar,
Proud to catch cold at a Venetian door;
Conscious they act a true Palladian part,
And, if they starve, they starve by rules of art.

   Oft have you hinted to your brother peer
A certain truth, which many buy too dear:
Something there is more needful than expense,
And something previous even to taste — 'tis sense:
Good sense, which only is the gift of Heaven,
And, though no science, fairly worth the seven:
A light, which in yourself you must perceive;
Jones and Le Nôtre have it not to give.

   To build, to plant, whatever you intend,
To rear the column, or the arch to bend,
To swell the terrace, or to sink the grot,
In all, let Nature never be forgot,
But treat the goddess like a modest fair,
Nor over-dress, nor leave her wholly bare;
Let not each beauty everywhere be spied,
Where half the skill is decently to hide.
He gains all points, who pleasingly confounds,
Surprises, varies, and conceals the bounds.

   Consult the genius of the place in all:
That tells the waters or to rise or fall;
Or helps the ambitious hill the heavens to scale,
Or scoops in circling theatres the vale;
Calls in the country, catches opening glades,
Joins willing woods, and varies shades from shades;
Now breaks, or now directs, the intending lines;

Paints, as you plant, and, as you work, designs.
Still follow sense, of every art the soul,
Parts answering parts shall slide into a whole,
Spontaneous beauties all around advance,
Start ev'n from difficulty, strike from chance;
Nature shall join you; Time shall make it grow
A work to wonder at — perhaps a Stowe.[23]
   Without it, proud Versailles! thy glory falls;
And Nero's terraces desert their walls:
The vast parterres a thousand hands shall make,
Lo! Cobham comes, and floats them with a lake:
Or cut wide views through mountains to the plain,
You'll wish your hill or shelter'd seat again.
Even in an ornament its place remark,
Nor in an hermitage set Dr. Clarke.[24]
Behold Villario's ten years' toil complete;
His quincunx darkens, his espaliers meet;
The wood supports the plain, the parts unite,
And strength of shade contends with strength of light;
A waving glow the bloomy beds display,
Blushing in bright diversities of day,
With silver-quivering rills meander'd o'er —
Enjoy them, you! Villario can no more:
Tired of the scene parterres and fountains yield,
He finds at last he better likes a field.
   Through his young woods how pleased Sabinus stray'd,
Or sate delighted in the thickening shade,
With annual joy the reddening shoots to greet,
Or see the stretching branches long to meet!
His son's fine taste an opener vista loves,
Foe to the Dryads of his father's groves;
One boundless green, or flourish'd carpet views,
With all the mournful family of yews:
The thriving plants, ignoble broomsticks made,
Now sweep those alleys they were born to shade.
   At Timon's villa let us pass a day,
Where all cry out, "What sums are thrown away!"

_____

[23] The home of Viscount Cobham.
[24] The theologian Samuel Clarke, whose bust was so placed by the Queen.

So proud, so grand: of that stupendous air,
Soft and agreeable come never there.
Greatness, with Timon, dwells in such a draught
As brings all Brobdignag before your thought.
To compass this, his building is a town,
His pond an ocean, his parterre a down:
Who but must laugh, the master when he sees,
A puny insect, shivering at a breeze!
Lo, what huge heaps of littleness around!
The whole, a labour'd quarry above ground,
Two cupids squirt before: a lake behind
Improves the keenness of the northern wind.
His gardens next your admiration call,
On every side you look, behold the wall!
No pleasing intricacies intervene,
No artful wildness to perplex the scene:
Grove nods at grove, each alley has a brother,
And half the platform just reflects the other.
The suffering eye inverted Nature sees,
Trees cut to statues, statues thick as trees;
With here a fountain, never to be play'd;
And there a summer-house, that knows no shade:
Here Amphitrite sails through myrtle bowers;
There gladiators fight, or die in flowers;
Unwater'd see the drooping sea-horse mourn,
And swallows roost in Nilus' dusty urn.
    My Lord advances with majestic mien,
Smit with the mighty pleasure to be seen:
But soft — by regular approach — not yet —
First through the length of yon hot terrace sweat;
And when up ten steep slopes you've dragg'd your thighs,
Just at his study-door he'll bless your eyes.
    His study! with what authors is it stored?
In books, not authors, curious is my Lord;
To all their dated backs he turns you round;
These Aldus printed, those Du Sueïl has bound.
Lo, some are vellum, and the rest as good
For all his Lordship knows, but they are wood.
For Locke or Milton 'tis in vain to look,
These shelves admit not any modern book.
    And now the chapel's silver bell you hear,

That summons you to all the pride of prayer:
Light quirks of music, broken and uneven,
Make the soul dance upon a jig to Heaven.
On painted ceilings you devoutly stare,
Where sprawl the saints of Verrio or Laguerre,
Or gilded clouds in fair expansion lie,
And bring all Paradise before your eye.
To rest, the cushion and soft dean invite,
Who never mentions Hell to ears polite.
    But hark! the chiming clocks to dinner call;
A hundred footsteps scrape the marble hall:
The rich buffet well-coloured serpents grace,
And gaping Tritons spew to wash your face.
Is this a dinner? this a genial room?
No, 'tis a temple, and a hecatomb.
A solemn sacrifice, perform'd in state,
You drink by measure, and to minutes eat.
So quick retires each flying course, you'd swear
Sancho's dread doctor and his wand were there.
Between each act the trembling salvers ring,
From soup to sweet-wine, and God bless the king.
In plenty starving, tantalised in state,
And complaisantly help'd to all I hate,
Treated, caress'd, and tired, I take my leave,
Sick of his civil pride from morn to eve;
I curse such lavish cost, and little skill,
And swear no day was ever pass'd so ill.
    Yet hence the poor are clothed, the hungry fed;
Health to himself, and to his infants bread,
The labourer bears: what his hard heart denies,
His charitable vanity supplies.
    Another age shall see the golden ear
Imbrown the slope, and nod on the parterre,
Deep harvest bury all his pride has plann'd,
And laughing Ceres reassume the land.
    Who then shall grace, or who improve the soil? —
Who plants like Bathurst,[25] or who builds like Boyle.
'Tis use alone that sanctifies expense,

---

[25] The first Earl Bathurst.

And splendour borrows all her rays from sense.
  His father's acres who enjoys in peace,
Or makes his neighbours glad, if he increase:
Whose cheerful tenants bless their yearly toil,
Yet to their lord owe more than to the soil;
Whose ample lawns are not ashamed to feed
The milky heifer and deserving steed;
Whose rising forests, not for pride or show,
But future buildings, future navies grow:
Let his plantations stretch from down to down,
First shade a country, and then raise a town.
  You too proceed! make falling arts your care,
Erect new wonders, and the old repair;
Jones and Palladio to themselves restore,
And be whate'er Vitruvius was before:
'Till kings call forth the ideas of your mind
(Proud to accomplish what such hands design'd),
Bid harbours open, public ways extend,
Bid temples, worthier of the god, ascend;
Bid the broad arch the dangerous flood contain,
The mole projected break the roaring main;
Back to his bounds their subject sea command,
And roll obedient rivers through the land;
These honours Peace to happy Britain brings,
These are imperial works, and worthy kings.

Epistle to Dr. Arbuthnot[26]

OR, PROLOGUE TO THE SATIRES

Neque sermonibus vulgi dederis te, nec in præmiis humanis spem posueris
rerum tuarum; suis te oportet illecebris ipsa virtus trahat ad verum decus. Quid
de te alii loquantur, ipsi videant, sed loquentur tamen. — Cicero
[And do not yield yourself up to the speeches of the vulgar, nor in your affairs
place hope in human rewards: virtue ought to draw you to true glory by its own
allurements. Why should others speak of you? Let them study themselves — yet
they will speak.]

---

[26] John Arbuthnot, humorist, friend of Pope.

Advertisement

This paper is a sort of bill of complaint, begun many years since, and drawn up by snatches, as the several occasions offered. I had no thoughts of publishing it, till it pleased some persons of rank and fortune (the authors of *Verses to the Imitator of Horace*, and of an *Epistle to a Doctor of Divinity from a Nobleman at Hampton Court*) to attack, in a very extraordinary manner, not only my writings (of which, being public, the public is judge), but my person, morals, and family, whereof, to those who know me not, a truer information may be requisite. Being divided between the necessity to say something of myself and my own laziness to undertake so awkward a task, I thought it the shortest way to put the last hand to this Epistle. If it have anything pleasing, it will be that by which I am most desirous to please, the truth and the sentiment; and if anything offensive, it will be only to those I am least sorry to offend, the vicious or the ungenerous.

Many will know their own pictures in it, there being not a circumstance but what is true; but I have for the most part spared their names, and they may escape being laughed at if they please.

I would have some of them know it was owing to the request of the learned and candid friend to whom it is inscribed that I make not as free use of theirs as they have done of mine. However, I shall have this advantage and honour on my side, that whereas, by their proceeding, any abuse may be directed at any man, no injury can possibly be done by mine, since a nameless character can never be found out but by its truth and likeness.

> *P.* Shut, shut the door, good John![27] fatigued, I said;
> Tie up the knocker, say I'm sick, I'm dead.
> The Dog-star rages! nay 'tis past a doubt,
> All Bedlam, or Parnassus, is let out:
> Fire in each eye, and papers in each hand,
> They rave, recite, and madden round the land.
>
> What walls can guard me, or what shades can hide?
> They pierce my thickets, through my grot they glide,
> By land, by water, they renew the charge,
> They stop the chariot, and they board the barge.
> No place is sacred, not the church is free,
> Ev'n Sunday shines no Sabbath-day to me:
> Then from the Mint[28] walks forth the man of rhyme,
> Happy! to catch me, just at dinner-time.
>
> Is there a parson, much bemused in beer,

---

[27] John Serle, Pope's servant.
[28] A sanctuary for insolvent debtors.

A maudlin poetess, a rhyming peer,
A clerk, foredoom'd his father's soul to cross,
Who pens a stanza, when he should engross?
Is there, who, lock'd from ink and paper, scrawls
With desperate charcoal round his darken'd walls?
All fly to Twit'nam,[29] and in humble strain
Apply to me, to keep them mad or vain.
Arthur,[30] whose giddy son neglects the laws,
Imputes to me and my damn'd works the cause:
Poor Cornus sees his frantic wife elope,
And curses wit, and poetry, and Pope.
      Friend to my life! (which did not you prolong,
The world had wanted many an idle song)
What drop or nostrum can this plague remove?
Or which must end me, a fool's wrath or love?
A dire dilemma! either way I'm sped,
If foes, they write, if friends, they read me dead.
Seized and tied down to judge, how wretched I!
Who can't be silent, and who will not lie:
To laugh, were want of goodness and of grace,
And to be grave, exceeds all power of face.
I sit with sad civility, I read
With honest anguish, and an aching head;
And drop at last, but in unwilling ears,
This saving counsel, — "Keep your piece nine years."
      "Nine years!" cries he, who, high in Drury Lane,
Lull'd by soft zephyrs through the broken pane,
Rhymes ere he wakes, and prints before Term ends,
Obliged by hunger, and request of friends:
"The piece, you think, is incorrect? why take it,
I'm all submission; what you'd have it, make it."
      Three things another's modest wishes bound,
My friendship, and a prologue, and ten pound.
      Pitholeon sends to me: "You know his grace,
I want a patron; ask him for a place."
Pitholeon libell'd me — "But here's a letter
Informs you, Sir, 'twas when he knew no better.

---

[29] Twickenham, where Pope lived.
[30] Arthur Moore, father of the poet James Moore (Smythe).

Dare you refuse him? Curll[31] invites to dine,
He'll write a journal, or he'll turn divine."
Bless me! a packet. "'Tis a stranger sues,
A virgin tragedy, an orphan Muse."
If I dislike it, "Furies, death and rage!"
If I approve, "Commend it to the stage."
There (thank my stars) my whole commission ends,
The players and I are, luckily, no friends;
Fired that the house reject him, "'Sdeath! I'll print it,
And shame the fools — Your interest, Sir, with Lintot."[32]
Lintot, dull rogue! will think your price too much:
"Not, Sir, if you revise it, and retouch."
All my demurs but double his attacks:
And last he whispers, "Do; and we go snacks."
Glad of a quarrel, straight I clap the door:
Sir, let me see your works and you no more.

  'Tis sung, when Midas' ears began to spring
(Midas, a sacred person and a king),
His very minister who spied them first
(Some say his queen) was forced to speak or burst:
And is not mine, my friend, a sorer case,
When every coxcomb perks them in my face?
  A. Good friend, forbear! you deal in dangerous things,
I'd never name queens, ministers, or kings:
Keep close to ears, and those let asses prick,
'Tis nothing — P. Nothing? if they bite and kick?
Out with it, DUNCIAD! let the secret pass,
That secret to each fool, that he's an ass:
The truth once told (and wherefore should we lie?)
The Queen of Midas slept, and so may I.
  You think this cruel? Take it for a rule,
No creature smarts so little as a fool.
Let peals of laughter, Codrus! round thee break,
Thou unconcerned canst hear the mighty crack:
Pit, box, and gallery in convulsions hurl'd,
Thou stand'st unshook amidst a bursting world.
Who shames a scribbler? break one cobweb through,

---

[31] Edmund Curll, bookseller, an adversary of Pope.
[32] Barnaby Bernard Lintot, one of Pope's publishers.

He spins the slight, self-pleasing thread anew:
Destroy his fib or sophistry, in vain,
The creature's at his dirty work again,
Throned in the centre of his thin designs,
Proud of a vast extent of flimsy lines!
Whom have I hurt? has poet yet, or peer,
Lost the arch'd eyebrow, or Parnassian sneer?
And has not Colley still his lord, and whore?
His butchers Henley,[33] his Freemasons Moore?[34]
Does not one table Bavius still admit?
Still to one bishop Philips seem a wit?
·Still Sappho — A. Hold! for God's sake — you'll offend:
No names — be calm — learn prudence of a friend.
I too could write, and I am twice as tall;
But foes like these — P. One flatterer's worse than all.
Of all mad creatures, if the learn'd are right,
It is the slaver kills, and not the bite.
A fool quite angry is quite innocent:
Alas! 'tis ten times worse when they repent.
    One dedicates in high heroic prose,
And ridicules beyond a hundred foes:
One from all Grub Street will my fame defend,
And, more abusive, calls himself my friend.
This prints my letters, that expects a bribe,
And others roar aloud, "Subscribe, subscribe!"
    There are, who to my person pay their court:
I cough like Horace, and, though lean, am short.
Ammon's great son one shoulder had too high —
Such Ovid's nose, — and, "Sir! you have an eye."
Go on, obliging creatures, make me see
All that disgraced my betters met in me.
Say, for my comfort, languishing in bed,
"Just so immortal Maro held his head";
And, when I die, be sure you let me know
Great Homer died three thousand years ago.
Why did I write? what sin to me unknown
Dipp'd me in ink, my parents', or my own?

---

[33] John Henley, the eccentric preacher who performed in markets.
[34] The poet mentioned in footnote 30 and later in this poem.

As yet a child, nor yet a fool to fame,
I lisp'd in numbers, for the numbers came.
I left no calling for this idle trade,
No duty broke, no father disobey'd:
The Muse but served to ease some friend, not wife,
To help me through this long disease, my life;
To second, ARBUTHNOT! thy art and care,
And teach the being you preserved to bear.
    But why then publish? Granville[35] the polite,
And knowing Walsh,[36] would tell me I could write;
Well-natured Garth[37] inflamed with early praise,
And Congreve loved, and Swift endured my lays;
The courtly Talbot,[38] Somers, Sheffield read,
Even mitred Rochester would nod the head,
And St. John's self (great Dryden's friend before)
With open arms received one poet more.
Happy my studies, when by these approved!
Happier their author, when by these beloved!
From these the world will judge of men and books,
Not from the Burnets, Oldmixons, and Cookes.[39]
    Soft were my numbers; who could take offence
While pure description held the place of sense?
Like gentle Fanny's was my flowery theme,
A painted mistress, or a purling stream.
Yet then did Gildon[39] draw his venal quill;
I wish'd the man a dinner, and sate still.
Yet then did Dennis rave in furious fret;
I never answer'd—I was not in debt.
If want provoked, or madness made them print,
I waged no war with Bedlam or the Mint.
    Did some more sober critic come abroad—
If wrong, I smiled; if right, I kiss'd the rod.
Pains, reading, study, are their just pretence,

---

[35] George Granville, Baron Lansdowne, patron of Pope.
[36] William Walsh, critic and poet.
[37] Sir Samuel Garth, physician and poet.
[38] Talbot, Somers, Sheffield, Rochester, Saint-John (Bolingbroke): highly placed admirers of Dryden and Pope.
[39] Burnet, Oldmixon, Cooke, Gildon: meretricious authors, enemies of Pope.

And all they want is spirit, taste, and sense.
Commas and points they set exactly right,
And 'twere a sin to rob them of their mite;
Yet ne'er one sprig of laurel graced these ribalds,
From slashing Bentley[40] down to piddling Tibbalds:[41]
Each wight, who reads not, and but scans and spells,
Each word-catcher, that lives on syllables,
Even such small critics, some regard may claim,
Preserved in Milton's or in Shakespeare's name.
Pretty! in amber to observe the forms
Of hairs, or straws, or dirt, or grubs, or worms!
The things, we know, are neither rich nor rare,
But wonder how the devil they got there.
    Were others angry — I excused them too;
Well might they rage, I gave them but their due.
A man's true merit 'tis not hard to find;
But each man's secret standard in his mind,
That casting-weight pride adds to emptiness,
This, who can gratify, for who can guess?
The bard whom pilfer'd Pastorals renown,
Who turns a Persian tale for half-a-crown,
Just writes to make his barrenness appear,
And strains from hard-bound brains, eight lines a-year;
He, who still wanting, though he lives on theft,
Steals much, spends little, yet has nothing left:
And he, who now to sense, now nonsense leaning,
Means not, but blunders round about a meaning:
And he, whose fustian's so sublimely bad,
It is not poetry, but prose run mad:
All these, my modest satire bade translate,
And own'd that nine such poets made a Tate.
How did they fume, and stamp, and roar, and chafe!
And swear, not Addison himself was safe.
    Peace to all such! but were there one whose fires
True genius kindles, and fair fame inspires;
Blest with each talent, and each art to please,
And born to write, converse, and live with ease;

---

[40] Richard Bentley, scholar and critic.
[41] Lewis Theobald, editor of Shakespeare, enemy of Pope.

Should such a man, too fond to rule alone,
Bear, like the Turk, no brother near the throne,
View him with scornful, yet with jealous eyes,
And hate for arts that caused himself to rise;
Damn with faint praise, assent with civil leer,
And, without sneering, teach the rest to sneer;
Willing to wound, and yet afraid to strike,
Just hint a fault, and hesitate dislike;
Alike reserved to blame, or to commend,
A timorous foe, and a suspicious friend;
Dreading e'en fools, by flatterers besieged,
And so obliging, that he ne'er obliged;
Like Cato, give his little senate laws,
And sit attentive to his own applause;
While wits and Templars every sentence raise,
And wonder with a foolish face of praise —
Who but must laugh, if such a man there be?
Who would not weep, if Atticus were he?

  What though my name stood rubric on the walls,
Or plaster'd posts, with claps, in capitals?
Or smoking forth, a hundred hawkers load,
On wings of winds came flying all abroad?
I sought no homage from the race that write;
I kept, like Asian monarchs, from their sight:
Poems I heeded (now be-rhym'd so long)
No more than thou, great George! a birthday song.
I ne'er with wits or witlings pass'd my days,
To spread about the itch of verse and praise;
Nor like a puppy, daggled through the town,
To fetch and carry, sing-song up and down;
Nor at rehearsals sweat, and mouth'd, and cried,
With handkerchief and orange at my side;
But sick of fops, and poetry, and prate,
To Bufo left the whole Castalian state.

  Proud as Apollo on his forked hill,
Sate full-blown Bufo, puff'd by every quill;
Fed with soft dedication all day long,
Horace and he went hand in hand in song.
His library (where busts of poets dead
And a true Pindar stood without a head)
Received of wits an undistinguish'd race,

Who first his judgment asked, and then a place:
Much they extoll'd his pictures, much his seat,
And flatter'd every day, and some days eat:
Till grown more frugal in his riper days,
He paid some bards with port, and some with praise,
To some a dry rehearsal was assign'd,
And others (harder still) he paid in kind.
Dryden alone (what wonder?) came not nigh,
Dryden alone escaped this judging eye:
But still the great have kindness in reserve,
He help'd to bury whom he help'd to starve.
　　May some choice patron bless each grey goose quill!
May every Bavius have his Bufo still!
So when a statesman wants a day's defence,
Or Envy holds a whole week's war with Sense,
Or simple pride for flattery makes demands,
May dunce by dunce be whistled off my hands!
Bless'd be the great! for those they take away,
And those they left me — for they left me GAY;
Left me to see neglected Genius bloom,
Neglected die, and tell it on his tomb:
Of all thy blameless life the sole return
My verse, and QUEENSBERRY weeping o'er thy urn!
　　Oh let me live my own, and die so too!
(To live and die is all I have to do:)
Maintain a poet's dignity and ease,
And see what friends, and read what books I please:
Above a patron, though I condescend
Sometimes to call a minister my friend.
I was not born for courts or great affairs:
I pay my debts, believe, and say my prayers;
Can sleep without a poem in my head,
Nor know if Dennis be alive or dead.
　　Why am I ask'd what next shall see the light?
Heavens! was I born for nothing but to write?
Has life no joys for me? or (to be grave)
Have I no friend to serve, no soul to save?
"I found him close with Swift — Indeed? no doubt
(Cries prating Balbus) something will come out."
'Tis all in vain, deny it as I will:
"No, such a genius never can lie still";

And then for mine obligingly mistakes
The first lampoon Sir Will[42] or Bubo makes.
Poor guiltless I! and can I choose but smile,
When every coxcomb knows me by my style?
    Cursed be the verse, how well soe'er it flow,
That tends to make one worthy man my foe,
Give Virtue scandal, Innocence a fear,
Or from the soft-eyed virgin steal a tear!
But he who hurts a harmless neighbour's peace,
Insults fall'n worth, or beauty in distress,
Who loves a lie, lame slander helps about,
Who writes a libel, or who copies out;
That fop, whose pride affects a patron's name,
Yet absent, wounds an author's honest fame;
Who can your merit selfishly approve,
And show the sense of it without the love;
Who has the vanity to call you friend,
Yet wants the honour, injured, to defend;
Who tells whate'er you think, whate'er you say,
And if he lie not, must at least betray;
Who to the dean and silver bell can swear,
And sees at Canons what was never there;
Who reads, but with a lust to misapply,
Makes satire a lampoon, and fiction lie;
A lash like mine no honest man shall dread,
But all such babbling blockheads in his stead.
    Let Sporus tremble —— A. What? that thing of silk,
Sporus, that mere white curd of ass's milk?
Satire or sense, alas! can Sporus feel,
Who breaks a butterfly upon a wheel?
    P. Yet let me flap this bug with gilded wings,
This painted child of dirt, that stinks and stings;
Whose buzz the witty and the fair annoys,
Yet wit ne'er tastes, and beauty ne'er enjoys:
So well-bred spaniels civilly delight
In mumbling of the game they dare not bite.
Eternal smiles his emptiness betray,
As shallow streams run dimpling all the way.

---

[42] Sir William Yonge, Secretary-at-War.

Whether in florid impotence he speaks,
And, as the prompter breathes, the puppet squeaks;
Or at the ear of Eve, familiar toad!
Half froth, half venom, spits himself abroad,
In puns, or politics, or tales, or lies,
Or spite, or smut, or rhymes, or blasphemies.
His wit all see-saw, between that and this,
Now high, now low, now master up, now miss,
And he himself one vile antithesis.
Amphibious thing! that acting either part,
The trifling head, or the corrupted heart;
Fop at the toilet, flatterer at the board,
Now trips a lady, and now struts a lord.
Eve's tempter thus the Rabbins have express'd,
A cherub's face, a reptile all the rest.
Beauty that shocks you, parts that none will trust,
Wit that can creep, and pride that licks the dust.
    Not Fortune's worshipper, nor Fashion's fool,
Not Lucre's madman, nor Ambition's tool,
Not proud, nor servile; be one poet's praise,
That, if he pleased, he pleased by manly ways:
That flattery, even to kings, he held a shame,
And thought a lie in verse or prose the same;
That not in Fancy's maze he wander'd long,
But stoop'd to Truth, and moralised his song:
That not for Fame, but Virtue's better end,
He stood the furious foe, the timid friend,
The damning critic, half-approving wit,
The coxcomb hit, or fearing to be hit;
Laughed at the loss of friends he never had,
The dull, the proud, the wicked, and the mad;
The distant threats of vengeance on his head,
The blow unfelt, the tear he never shed;
The tale revived, the lie so oft o'erthrown,
Th' imputed trash, and dulness not his own;
The morals blacken'd when the writings 'scape,
The libell'd person, and the pictured shape;
Abuse, on all he loved, or loved him, spread,
A friend in exile, or a father dead;
The whisper, that to greatness still too near,
Perhaps yet vibrates on his sovereign's ear —

Welcome for thee, fair Virtue! all the past:
For thee, fair Virtue! welcome even the last!
 A. But why insult the poor, affront the great?
 P. A knave's a knave, to me, in every state;
Alike my scorn, if he succeed or fail,
Sporus at court, or Japhet in a jail,[43]
A hireling scribbler, or a hireling peer,
Knight of the post corrupt, or of the shire;
If on a pillory, or near a throne,
He gain his prince's ear, or lose his own.
 Yet soft by nature, more a dupe than wit,
Sappho can tell you how this man was bit:
This dreaded satirist Dennis will confess
Foe to his pride, but friend to his distress:
So humble, he has knocked at Tibbald's door,
Has drunk with Cibber, nay has rhymed for Moore.
Full ten years slander'd, did he once reply?
Three thousand suns went down on Welsted's[44] lie;
To please a mistress one aspersed his life;
He lash'd him not, but let her be his wife:
Let Budgell[45] charge low Grub Street on his quill,
And write whate'er he pleased, except his will;
Let the two Curlls of town and court abuse
His father, mother, body, soul, and Muse.
Yet why? that father held it for a rule,
It was a sin to call our neighbour fool:
That harmless mother thought no wife a whore:
Hear this, and spare his family, James Moore!
Unspotted names, and memorable long!
If there be force in virtue, or in song.
 Of gentle blood (part shed in honour's cause,
While yet in Britain honour had applause)
Each parent sprung—A. What fortune, pray?—P. Their own,
And better got, than Bestia's from the throne.
Born to no pride, inheriting no strife,
Nor marrying discord in a noble wife,

---

43 Japhet Crook, the forger.
44 Leonard Welsted, poet, enemy of Pope.
45 Eustace Budgell, writer.

Stranger to civil and religious rage,
The good man walk'd innoxious through his age.
No courts he saw, no suits would ever try,
Nor dared an oath, nor hazarded a lie.
Unlearn'd, he knew no schoolman's subtle art,
No language, but the language of the heart.
By nature honest, by experience wise,
Healthy by temperance, and by exercise,
His life, though long, to sickness pass'd unknown,
His death was instant, and without a groan.
O grant me thus to live, and thus to die!
Who sprung from kings shall know less joy than I.
    O friend! may each domestic bliss be thine!
Be no unpleasing melancholy mine:
Me, let the tender office long engage,
To rock the cradle of reposing age,
With lenient arts extend a mother' breath,
Make languor smile, and smooth the bed of death.
Explore the thought, explain the asking eye,
And keep awhile one parent from the sky!
On cares like these if length of days attend,
May Heaven, to bless those days, preserve my friend,
Preserve him social, cheerful, and serene,
And just as rich as when he served a queen.
    A. Whether that blessing be denied or given,
Thus far was right, the rest belongs to Heaven.

Epigram

Engraved on the Collar of a Dog Which I Gave to His Royal Highness[46]

I am his Highness' dog at Kew;
Pray tell me, sir, whose dog are you?

---

[46] Frederick, Prince of Wales, father of George III.

Alphabetical List of Titles

Alphabetical List of First Lines

DOVER · THRIFT · EDITIONS

POETRY

THE CONGO AND OTHER POEMS, Vachel Lindsay. 96pp. 0-486-27272-9

EVANGELINE AND OTHER POEMS, Henry Wadsworth Longfellow. 64pp. 0-486-28255-4

FAVORITE POEMS, Henry Wadsworth Longfellow. 96pp. 0-486-27273-7

COMPLETE POEMS, Christopher Marlowe. 112pp. 0-486-42674-2

"TO HIS COY MISTRESS" AND OTHER POEMS, Andrew Marvell. 64pp. 0-486-29544-3

SPOON RIVER ANTHOLOGY, Edgar Lee Masters. 144pp. 0-486-27275-3

SELECTED POEMS, Claude McKay. 80pp. 0-486-40876-0

SONGS OF MILAREPA, Milarepa. 128pp. 0-486-42814-1

RENASCENCE AND OTHER POEMS, Edna St. Vincent Millay. 64pp. (Not available in Europe or the United Kingdom) 0-486-26873-X

SELECTED POEMS, John Milton. 128pp. 0-486-27554-X

CIVIL WAR POETRY: An Anthology, Paul Negri (ed.). 128pp. 0-486-29883-3

ENGLISH VICTORIAN POETRY: AN ANTHOLOGY, Paul Negri (ed.). 256pp. 0-486-40425-0

GREAT SONNETS, Paul Negri (ed.). 96pp. 0-486-28052-7

THE RAVEN AND OTHER FAVORITE POEMS, Edgar Allan Poe. 64pp. 0-486-26685-0

ESSAY ON MAN AND OTHER POEMS, Alexander Pope. 128pp. 0-486-28053-5

GOBLIN MARKET AND OTHER POEMS, Christina Rossetti. 64pp. 0-486-28055-1

CHICAGO POEMS, Carl Sandburg. 80pp. 0-486-28057-8

CORNHUSKERS, Carl Sandburg. 157pp. 0-486-41409-4

COMPLETE SONNETS, William Shakespeare. 80pp. 0-486-26686-9

SELECTED POEMS, Percy Bysshe Shelley. 128pp. 0-486-27558-2

AFRICAN-AMERICAN POETRY: An Anthology, 1773–1930, Joan R. Sherman (ed.). 96pp. 0-486-29604-0

NATIVE AMERICAN SONGS AND POEMS: An Anthology, Brian Swann (ed.). 64pp. 0-486-29450-1

SELECTED POEMS, Alfred Lord Tennyson. 112pp. 0-486-27282-6

AENEID, Vergil (Publius Vergilius Maro). 256pp. 0-486-28749-1

GREAT LOVE POEMS, Shane Weller (ed.). 128pp. 0-486-27284-2

CIVIL WAR POETRY AND PROSE, Walt Whitman. 96pp. 0-486-28507-3

SELECTED POEMS, Walt Whitman. 128pp. 0-486-26878-0

THE BALLAD OF READING GAOL AND OTHER POEMS, Oscar Wilde. 64pp. 0-486-27072-6

EARLY POEMS, William Carlos Williams. 64pp. (Available in U.S. only.) 0-486-29294-0

FAVORITE POEMS, William Wordsworth. 80pp. 0-486-27073-4

EARLY POEMS, William Butler Yeats. 128pp. 0-486-27808-5